THE BOY IN TH
PAJAM

John Boyne

AUTHORED by Meghan Joyce Tozer
UPDATED AND REVISED by Aaron Suduiko

COVER DESIGN by Table XI Partners LLC
COVER PHOTO by Olivia Verma and © 2005 GradeSaver, LLC

BOOK DESIGN by Table XI Partners LLC

Published by GradeSaver LLC, www.gradesaver.com

First published in the United States of America by GradeSaver LLC. 2014

ISBN 978-1-60259-465-4

Printed in the United States of America

For other products and additional information please visit http://www.gradesaver.com

Table of Contents

Biography of John Boyne (1971–)

John Boyne was born on April 30, 1971 in Ireland. He earned his undergraduate degree in English Literature from Trinity College in Dublin, and later attended the University of East Anglia in Norwich for his Masters degree in creative writing.

Although Boyne has not yet written a novel set in his home country, he has said in multiple interviews that he strongly identifies as an Irish writer. He cites two of his strongest influences as Charles Dickens and John Irving. Boyne has published about seventy short stories, including most of his earliest works. His first story, "The Entertainments Jar," was published in *The Sunday Tribune* when Boyne was just twenty-one years old. In 2007, he challenged himself to write a series of fifty "short short stories," one per week, for *The Sunday Tribune.* Each story was just 500 words long.

In 2000, he published his first novel, *The Thief of Time*. Since then, he has published seven more adult novels, including *Crippen* (2004), which some critics found to be misogynistic. This criticism bothered Boyne, who took care to create deeper female characters in *The Boy in the Striped Pajamas.*

In addition to *The Boy in the Striped Pajamas*, which was his first young adult novel, Boyne has published three other books for young readers: *Noah Barleywater Runs Away* (2010), *The Terrible Thing That Happened to Barnaby Brocket* (2012), and *Stay Where You Are and Then Leave* (2013).

Boyne was inducted into the Hennessy Literary Awards Hall of Fame in 2012.

The Boy in the Striped Pajamas Summary

Bruno, a young boy living in Berlin during the Nazi regime, arrives home from school one day to find his family's maid, Maria, packing up his things. When he asks his mother what is going on, she explains that Bruno's father's job is the reason they are all leaving their home in Berlin; someone Bruno knows only as "the Fury" has plans for his father's career. Chapter Two begins with a comparison of Bruno's old home in Berlin to his new living situation. In contrast to his family's big, beautiful home in Berlin, "there was something about the new house that made Bruno think that no one ever laughed there; that there was nothing to laugh at and nothing to be happy about" (13).

Chapter Three introduces Gretel, Bruno's older sister by three years, whom he refers to as "Trouble From Day One" (21). Bruno runs into Gretel's room and discovers her arranging her dolls around her room. She agrees with Bruno that their new living situation is horrible and tells him that the place is called "Out-With." Bruno shows Gretel the scene from his bedroom window: There are boys, men, and elderly men living together on the opposite side of a fence that extends farther than they can see into the distance. After Gretel returns to her room, Bruno continues to watch the people out his bedroom window and notices that they're all wearing the same thing: "a pair of grey striped pajamas with a grey striped cap on their heads" (38).

Bruno decides to speak to Father, who arrived at Out-With a few days earlier. When Bruno asks when they can return to Berlin, Father tells him to give Out-With a chance, because it is their home now, "for the foreseeable future" (48). Before he leaves, Bruno asks Father who the people are outside his window. Father answers, "Those people... well, they're not people at all, Bruno... at least not as we understand the term" (53). A few days later, Bruno engages Maria in conversation, hoping she will agree with him that Out-With is a horrible place, but she avoids saying anything negative. She hints that she cannot understand how such a good man could be doing Father's job at Out-With.

Several weeks go by and Bruno is bored at Out-With, so he builds a rope swing and a couple of hours later, falls off of it. He injures himself, scraping up his knee pretty badly. Pavel, one of the prisoners at Out-With who works in the family's home as a waiter, sees the whole thing and runs out to help Bruno. Since Mother is still not home, Pavel cleans Bruno's wounds in the kitchen and tells Bruno that he used to be a doctor. When Mother arrives home, she tells Bruno to go to his room and he overhears her saying to Pavel, "If the Commandant Asks, we'll say that I cleaned Bruno up" (85).

More than anyone else from Berlin, Bruno misses his Grandfather and Grandmother. His Grandfather had run a restaurant in the town center, and his Grandmother had been a famous singer. The last time he saw them in Berlin, Grandmother had become outraged at Father's new promotion. She had stormed out of their house, and Bruno hadn't seen her since. He decides to write her a letter from Out-With, telling her how unhappy he is in their new home and how much he misses her.

Father decides to hire a man named Herr Liszt as a tutor for Gretel and Bruno. Herr Liszt focuses on history and geography, neither of which is very interesting to Bruno, but the tutor insists that he learn about "The Fatherland" (98). A few days later, Bruno gets the urge to go exploring and decides to walk along the fence as far as he can, although Mother and Father have told him many times that exploration is banned at Out-With. Right when he starts feeling hungry and begins to think about turning back, he sees a little boy on the other side of the fence, wearing the striped pajamas that all people on the other side of the fence wear. Bruno is "sure that he had never seen a skinnier or sadder boy in his life" (107). Bruno strikes up a conversation with the boy, whose name is Shmuel, sitting down on his own side of the fence so he can talk through it. Shmuel is from Poland and Bruno tells him that, "Germany is the greatest of all countries... We're superior" (112), but even as he says this, he realizes that his words sound rude.

Chapter Eleven takes the form of a flashback to a few months earlier, when Bruno's family still lived in Berlin. One night, the Fury had come to their home for dinner with a kind woman named Eva. After the Fury and Eva had left, Bruno had overheard his parents' conversation about leaving Berlin. Days later, he had arrived home from school to find Maria packing his belongings.

Chapter Twelve returns to Bruno and Shmuel's conversation from opposite sides of the fence. Shmuel explains how he came to live at Out-With. His family was told they had to move to a different part of Cracow, on the wrong side of a wall that soldiers built, all cramped in one room with another family. One day soldiers arrived and packed him and everyone living nearby into huge trucks, and later into a train with no doors. Shmuel tells Bruno that there are hundreds of other boys on his side of the fence, and Bruno reiterates his feeling that it is unfair for him to have no one to play with on *his* side. Weeks pass and Bruno visits with his new friend Shmuel regularly.

One evening, Lieutenant Kotler joins Bruno's family for dinner. Lieutenant Kotler mentions that his father was a professor of literature at the university, but that he had left Germany for Switzerland in 1938. This information embarrasses Lieutenant Kotler and disturbs Father, who comments with suspicion that it is "[strange] that he chose not to stay in the Fatherland" (146). Pavel uncorks a new bottle of wine and accidentally spills it on Lieutenant Kotler because his hands are shaking. Lieutenant Kotler reacts very angrily and violently, although the details of his actions against Pavel are not revealed. Bruno goes to bed extremely upset about what happened to Pavel.

One rainy day, Bruno accidentally mentions Shmuel to Gretel but quickly covers it up, explaining that Shmuel is the name of his imaginary friend. The rain continues on and off for the next few weeks, during which Bruno is unable to meet with Shmuel as often as he would like. Mother is planning a birthday party for Father and

Lieutenant Kotler is spending a lot of time at the house with her; they are having an affair. On the day before the party, Bruno finds Shmuel in the kitchen; Lieutenant Kotler has brought him there because his hands are small enough to polish the glasses for Father's birthday party. Bruno begins to help himself to some cold chicken and stuffing that's in the refrigerator and when he sees Shmuel looking at the food, he offers his friend some. Lieutenant Kotler returns and accuses Shmuel of stealing food to eat. When Shmuel tells him that Bruno gave it to him and that Bruno is his friend, but Bruno is frightened and denies it. Bruno leaves the kitchen feeling incredibly guilty about having betrayed his friend. For almost a week, Shmuel does not come back to meet him at the fence and when he finally returns, his face is covered in bruises. Bruno apologizes for letting him down and says he's ashamed of himself. Shmuel smiles and forgives him, lifting up the fence so that they can shake hands beneath it.

The family receives news that Grandmother has died, so they return to their old home in Berlin for two days to attend the funeral. The two days are so sad that Bruno is almost relieved to return to Out-With. Lieutenant Kotler has been suddenly transferred away from Out-With, coinciding with a huge fight between Mother and Father. Bruno decides to ask Gretel about why he and Shmuel have to live on opposite sides of the fence. She explains that the people on the other side of the fence are Jews and that the fence is there to keep them from getting out and mixing with anyone else. When Bruno asks her what he and their family are, if not Jews, she says simply that they're "the opposite" (183). While they are talking, it is revealed that Gretel and Bruno both have lice. They treat their hair with a special shampoo, but then Father goes a step further and insists that Bruno have all his hair shaved off; Bruno notices that this makes him look even more like Shmuel. A few weeks later, Father calls Gretel and Bruno into his office and tells them that the Fury will not relieve him of his command, but that Mother wants to go back to Berlin immediately. Preparations begin so that Mother, Gretel, and Bruno can return to Berlin that week, but Bruno is nervous about telling Shmuel the news.

Bruno tells Shmuel that he is returning to Berlin. Shmuel is saddened by this news, and suggests that he come over to the other side of the fence. They decide that the next day, Shmuel will bring him a pair of striped pajamas, and he will sneak over to the other side of the fence to help Shmuel search for his father. The next day is rainy and muddy, but Bruno goes to meet Shmuel, who has brought with him a pair of dirty-looking striped pajamas. He hands the pajamas under the fence to Bruno, who carefully changes into them, leaving his own clothes in a pile in the mud. Shmuel lifts the fence and Bruno shimmies underneath it, becoming quite muddy in the process. In contrast to what Bruno had envisioned, the people on the other side of the fence are just standing or sitting, "looking horribly sad" (207). They are all too skinny and have shaved heads, which Bruno takes to indicate they have had lice here, too. The boys spend an hour and a half searching for evidence of where Shmuel's father could have gone. They don't find anything, which is what Shmuel had expected, and Bruno says again that he ought to go home. Just then, the soldiers round up the people around Bruno and Shmuel. Shmuel reassures Bruno that "it happens sometimes... They make people go on marches" (210). Just as Bruno is beginning to lose patience and deciding that he really must go home because he is too cold, the group is marched into a warm, airtight room. Bruno apologizes to Shmuel that they weren't able to find his father and tells him that he is his "best friend for life" (213). At that moment, the people in the room with them all gasp as the door is slammed shut and locked. The room becomes dark and chaotic, but Bruno and Shmuel continue to hold hands.

The soldiers search for Bruno for days before the pile of his clothes and boots is discovered by the fence. Father goes to see them but cannot figure out what happened to his son. Mother and Gretel stay at Out-With for a few months waiting for news of Bruno. One day, Mother has the sudden notion that he might have returned to their home in Berlin, so she rushes back with Gretel but doesn't find Bruno there. Over the next year, Father becomes very disliked by all the soldiers at Out-With. The finally, he returns to the place where his son's clothes had been found and notices the opening in the fence. He realizes what must have happened, and a few months later he is discharged from his post at Out-With and taken away by soldiers.

The Boy in the Striped Pajamas Background

The Boy in the Striped Pajamas, published in the United Kingdom with the alternate spelling *The Boy in the Striped Pyjamas*, won many international and Irish awards, including two Irish Book Awards and the Bisto Book of the Year. It topped the New York Times Bestseller List and has sold over 50 million copies worldwide. The book was rank first in Ireland for over 80 weeks and was the bestselling book in Spain for two years.

Boyne had always been fascinated by the Holocaust and had studied the historical context of the genocide and World War II. He reports that within 100 hours of having the initial idea to write a novel set during the Holocaust, he had completed the first draft of *The Boy in the Striped Pajamas*. The ending of the novel was set in stone from that first draft, completed on April 30, 2004.

The Boy in the Striped Pajamas is described on the title page as "a fable," a characterization Boyne has said he chose in order to explain some of the story's unrealistic aspects. In interviews, the author stresses that rather than being a historical novel about Auschwitz, the book is meant to be a universal story about any concentration camp in World War II, since so many children were victimized during that time. He gives this as the reason the name "Auschwitz" never appears in the novel; rather, the reader only gets Bruno's mishearing of the name, "Out With."

Bruno's confusion surrounding the situation at "Out With" is an example of Boyne's technique of defamiliarization. Through the voice of a limited, third-person narrator, Boyne leads the reader to Auschwitz and introduces the terrible things taking place there as if the reader has no prior knowledge on the topic. This allows the reader to avoid immediately categorizing the victims of the Holocaust as "Others," fundamentally different and unknowable. Rather, the reader gains the perspective of Bruno's childlike innocence.

By characterizing *The Boy in the Striped Pajamas* as a fable, Boyne avoids the retrospective speculation that often marks Holocaust novels. Rather, he implies that Bruno's story is an allegory, serving as a timeless representation of atrocities and the people who participate in and/or become victims of them. It poses the question whether perpetrators of such horrors as the Holocaust might rethink their behavior if they were to themselves become a victim of the horror - as in what happens to Bruno's father.

The book is an example of a trend in children's literature that acknowledges the extent to which children can be witnesses and victims of issues much larger than themselves. Though the Holocaust and all its atrocities are outside the realm of Bruno's understanding as a child, he and his family are participants and he becomes a victim by the end of the novel.

Growing up in war-torn Ireland, Boyne has said he felt a personal connection to the story of *The Boy in the Striped Pajamas.* This connection is revealed in certain details: for example, the characters of Bruno and Schmuel share a birthday, among other similarities. The specific date, April 15, 1934, is Boyne's father's birthday.

The Boy in the Striped Pajamas Characters

Bruno

The nine-year-old protagonist of the story. He moves with his family from their home in Berlin to Out-With, where Father has taken a new job.

Maria

The maid who moves to Out-With with Bruno's family. Her mother worked as Father's mother's seamstress, and Father offered her a job when she was destitute.

Mother

Bruno and Gretl's mother is "a tall woman with long red hair" (1) who quietly resents having to move her family to Out-With.

Lars

The butler for Bruno's family while they live in Berlin.

The Fury

Bruno's mishearing of the Furor, or Adolf Hitler. He is Father's boss and appoints Father to work at Out-With. Bruno meets the Fury when he and Eva come to dinner at Bruno's family's home in Berlin. He is described as "far shorter than Father" with "dark hair, which was cut quite short, and a tiny moustache" (121). Bruno finds him very rude.

Karl

One of Bruno's school friends in Berlin, whose father is a greengrocer.

Daniel

One of Bruno's school friends in Berlin, whose father is a teacher.

Martin

One of Bruno's school friends in Berlin, whose father is a chef.

Pavel

An old man who prepares meals and waits on Bruno's family at Out-With. He is a former doctor and now a prisoner at Out-With. He is described as "quite a small man, and very skinny too, with long fingers and angular features" (83).

Lieutenant Kotler

One of the Nazi soldiers stationed at Out-With. He has "very blonde hair, an almost unnatural shade of yellow" (18). Gretl develops a crush on him, and it is implied that he is carrying on an affair with Mother. He is cruel and Bruno doesn't like him.

Gretel

Bruno's older sister, who is twelve years old when the story begins. Over the course of the story, she goes from playing with her dolls all day to keeping track of the progress of the war with maps and studying German history.

Hilda

One of Gretel's school friends in Berlin.

Isobel

One of Gretel's school friends in Berlin.

Louise

One of Gretel's school friends in Berlin.

Herr Roller

A man whom Bruno remembers as being mad, who lived on the same street as his family in Berlin. Mother tells Bruno that before suffering a head injury during the Great War, Herr Roller had loved to dance.

Herr Liszt

The tutor whom Father hires to teach Gretl and Bruno about German history and geography. He is determined to indoctrinate the children with the ideas of the Nazi party.

Grandfather

Bruno's father's father ran a restaurant in the center of Berlin for most of his life. He was supportive of Father's promotion to Commandant.

Grandmother

Bruno's father's mother is sixty-two with "long red hair and green eyes" (87). She is a retired singer and when Bruno's family lived in Berlin, she would put on plays with Gretl and Bruno during parties. She is furious to find out about Father's promotion to Commandant and storms out of the house during a Christmas party.

Shmuel

The boy Bruno meets through the fence at Out-With. He is a prisoner and must wear the "striped pajamas" all the other prisoners wear. He shares a birthday with Bruno and they become friends.

Luka

One of the boys in the family that shared a one-room apartment with Shmuel's family in the Cracow ghetto. He physically bullied Shmuel.

Josef

Shmuel's brother.

Eva

The woman who accompanies the Fury to dinner at Bruno's family's home in Berlin. Bruno describes her as "quite the most beautiful woman he had ever seen in his life," with "blonde hair and very red lips" (121). She is based on the real-life Eva Braun, Hitler's long-time companion.

Father

As the story begins, Bruno's father has been appointed to run Auschwitz. He is kind to Bruno and Gretel but cruel and narrow-minded.

The Boy in the Striped Pajamas Glossary

bales

large bundles or packages, prepared for shipping or storage by being bound together with wire or cords.

boneshaker

a rickety vehicle.

buffet

to strike with the hand or fist.

commandant

the commanding officer of a place or group.

ergo

therefore.

flounce

to go with exaggerated, dramatic movements of the body.

forlorn

lonely, miserable, or desolate.

grimace

a disapproving or pained facial expression.

implant

to put firmly.

inconsolable

unable to be comforted.

incumbent

currently holding a role or position.

peckish

slightly hungry, and irritable as a result of this.

senile

declining in mental functioning as a result of old age.

sheik

the patriarch or chief of a tribe.

simper

to smile self-consciously.

squelch

to put down or suppress with crushing force.

tartan

a wool cloth worn by Scottish Highlander clans, each having a distinctive plaid pattern.

torrent

a rushing, violent stream of water.

trek

a difficult journey.

tubercular

having tuberculosis, an infectious disease affecting the lungs.

The Boy in the Striped Pajamas Themes

Gender inequality

Boyne concerns himself with the plight of female characters, though the details of their specific situations are revealed through the lens of Bruno's narration. Father's literal silencing of Mother in most of their conversations is representative of the figurative silencing of women's voices at this point in history, as well as in many times of war. At first, Mother reacts passive aggressively, the only way she can, for example by referring to Father as "some people." When Bruno overhears Mother confronting Father in Chapter Seventeen, she speaks up for herself and demands to leave Out-With. She tells Father, "This is your assignment, not ours. You stay if you want to" (187). At a time when gender roles determined that a wife obey her husband, this distinction between his responsibilities and her own is a bold statement.

Grandmother is outspoken about her strong disapproval of Father's new appointment to Commandant and represents the strongest voice among the female characters, who are the only ones with reservations about what is going on in their country. Maria must keep her silence because of her financial dependence on Bruno's Father and Mother makes small defiant gestures like protecting Pavel, but Grandmother spoke up loud and clear about her disapproval. Unfortunately, because of her position as a woman, she is unable to do anything to stop her son from pursuing his career in the Nazi party.

Childlike Misunderstanding of Tragedy

One of the ways Boyne establishes that the third-person narration is from Bruno's childish point of view is through the use of capitalization and misnaming of specific, recognizable names. For example, Bruno refers to his father's boss as "the Fury"; the reader must extrapolate that this is actually "the Furor," or Adolf Hitler. When Father prompts him to shout "Heil Hitler!" upon leaving the office at the end of Chapter Five, Bruno assumes this notorious Nazi salute is just "another way of saying, 'Well, goodbye for now, have a pleasant afternoon'" (54). Bruno understands that Father's office is "Out Of Bounds At All Times And No Exceptions," a phrase that he has memorized after hearing it many times from his parents, the reader imagines. Bruno's sister, Gretel, is introduced as being "Trouble From Day One" (21). This way of thinking about things so concretely, of making sense of a rule and applying it to all situations, is a characteristic of Bruno that identifies him as a child. The reader is encouraged to take on this childlike point of view through the use of capitalization. Because of the limits of the narrator, the reader is able to approach the horrors of the

Holocaust as if he or she has no prior knowledge - much like Bruno. The reader is required to put together details Bruno notices in order to make sense of the larger issues at play.

Timelessness of War and Genocide

In Chapter Three, Gretel tells Bruno that the place they are now living is called "Out-With," and this is what he continues to call it from this point on in the story. It is clearly a misunderstanding of the name "Auschwitz," but by not referring to the concentration camp by its proper name, Boyne avoids specificity to a certain extent. Bruno doesn't understand the derogatory term that Lieutenant Kotler calls Pavel and, later, Shmuel. By not specifically naming the word, Boyne both allows the reader to take on Bruno's childlike perspective and suggests the universality of this interaction. Lieutenant Kotler could be any soldier during any war time, shouting a derogatory term to dehumanize a victim of any genocide. This allows the fable a sense of timelessness, extending beyond the specific situation at Auschwitz.

In the last chapters, Boyne issues a veiled call to action to the reader, who could be living during a time of war or genocide. The most obvious instance is in the ironic tone on the final page of the story, after a devastated Father has been taken away from Out-With: "Of course all this happened a long time ago and nothing like that could ever happen again. Not in this day and age" (216). Boyne means for the reader to consider just the opposite: there are genocides occurring in this day and age, all over the world, and the reader is likely employing various coping strategies to ignore or dismiss them. Bruno's annoyance at being forced to march with the group of Jews in the concentration camp is representative of the disconnect many witnesses to genocide experience. As he is marched through the cold mud and rain, "he longed to be back in his house, watching all this from a distance and not wrapped up in the center of it" (211). This idea is a commentary on the perspective of those who allowed the Holocaust to occur while they remained removed from it, since it did not affect them personally. It applies to all witnesses to genocide in any time or place. The reader is meant to question how easy it is to watch "from a distance," as long as one is not victimized.

Indoctrination

The indoctrination of children employed by the Nazi party is most obvious in the character of Gretel. When we first meet her in Chapter Three, she is clearly a child, though a few years older than Bruno. She spends most of her time arranging her dolls and has brought the entire collection from Berlin with her. Significantly, she is the one who tells Bruno that the name of their new home is "Out-With." This misnaming of the specific location marks Gretel as a child at this point, in contrast to the teenager she will grow into by the end of the story. When Bruno points out how young she is in front of Lieutenant Kotler, she responds by snapping at him, "'I'll be thirteen in a couple of weeks' time. A teenager. Just like you'" (74). Her words to

Lieutenant Kotler accomplish two things: first, they foreshadow her mental shift as she grows out of childhood; and second, they remind the reader that some of the Nazi soldiers committing horrible actions against the Jews in the concentration camps were indoctrinated teenagers. Finally, Gretel replaces her collection of dolls with maps of Europe given to her by Father, which she updates using the newspapers each day as she reads about developments in the war. Her transition out of childhood naivete is represented clearly in her correction of Bruno's usage of "Out-With" in place for "Auschwitz." It was she who first told him the name of the place, but now she corrects him. Her understanding of the situation is still simplistic and lacks understanding: she has accepted what her Father and Herr Liszt have taught her without much critical thinking.

Natural vs. Unnatural

The theme of unnaturalness, especially as it relates to Auschwitz and the Holocaust generally, is introduced in Chapter Six. Instead of answering Bruno's question about whether she likes it at Out-With, Maria describes how much she loved the garden at the house in Berlin. Bruno takes this as an indirect answer to his question, since it is in such stark contrast to the atmosphere at Auschwitz. The theme of the Holocaust being unnatural arises again in Chapter Eleven, when Mother protests the move to Out-With by saying, "...as if it's the most natural thing in the world and it's not, it's just not..." (124). The Nazis used the argument that the Aryan race was "naturally" superior to all others, using the idea of natural dominance as justification in exterminating the Jewish population. But Boyne turns this assumption on its head, pointing out throughout the story just how "unnatural" the atmosphere and situation at Out-With really is.

Justification of Evil Actions

Boyne embeds questions and key ideas about the nature of human interaction into the characters' conversations in order to draw the reader's attention to larger issues. For example, Father assures Bruno that the Jews on the other side of the fence are "not people at all" - this is how he justifies to himself killing them at Auschwitz (53).

Maria's description of how kind Father has been to her serves as a commentary on the mental and emotional justification for Nazi soldiers generally, who might do kind deeds and appear to be wonderful people in other parts of their lives, while simultaneously carrying out the extermination of Jews.

Complacency

Bruno's betrayal of Shmuel in front of Lieutenant Kotler is representative of the many people who betrayed their Jewish neighbors and friends during the Holocaust in similar ways, by simply being complacent. By distancing himself from Shmuel because he is afraid of the consequences of associating with the boy, Bruno contributes to Shmuel's punishment for a crime he did not commit: stealing food. The way Bruno considers his actions immediately following the event reflects a personal disconnect: "He wondered how a boy who thought he was a good person really could act in such a cowardly way toward a friend" (174). He feels ashamed of himself, but does not take action to right the wrong. When Shmuel finally returns to meet him at the fence, his face covered in bruises, Bruno apologizes. His words could have easily come from any of the Germans who fell in line with the Nazis and didn't speak up for the Jews during the Holocaust.

Another example of the theme of complacency is when Lieutenant Kotler attacks Pavel for accidentally spilling the wine on him. The narrator only states that, "What happened then was both unexpected and extremely unpleasant. Lieutenant Kotler grew very angry with Pavel and no one - not Bruno, not Gretel, not Mother and not even Father - stepped in to stop him doing what he did next, even though none of them could watch" (148-49). This omission of detail makes the interaction representative of all acts of violence against Jews at the hands of Nazis and, in fact, against the oppressed group in any genocide throughout history. Bruno and his family represent the bystanders who were repulsed by did not act to stop the violence.

Arbitrary Boundaries

The most obvious boundary in the story is the fence dividing Bruno's side of Out-With from Shmuel's side. But Boyne calls into question the arbitrary boundaries that got each boy to his side of the fence: most importantly, that between Jews and "Opposites." Shmuel serves as a mirror character for Bruno; they were born on the same day, and Bruno declares, "We're like twins" (110). The symbols of the Star of David and the Nazi Swastika, which are never named, come to represent the arbitrary boundary that allowed the Nazis to exterminate other human beings. In Chapter Twelve, Shmuel describes how he came to have to wear his Star of David armband and draws the symbol in the dirt. Bruno points out that his Father wears one, too, and draws the Nazi symbol in the dirt on his side of the fence. The key difference between them is that Shmuel is Jewish and thus a member of the oppressed group in this genocide, while Bruno happens to be German and thus a member of the oppressing group. When Bruno tells Shmuel that Father also wears an armband, Shmuel observes, "Yes, but they're different, aren't they?" (127).

The use of Shmuel's point of view further blurs the boundary between the two boys. When Bruno has put on the pajamas and turns around to show Shmuel what he looks like, "It was almost (Shmuel thought) as if they were all exactly the same really" (204). Boyne puts the indication of Shmuel's point of view in parentheses in order to imply that while the thought is Shmuel's, it is also a commentary on the situation generally. Once Bruno puts on the pajamas he looks no different from Shmuel, but really, the distinction made between the Jews and the Germans is arbitrary and erroneous, since they are all human beings.

Human Nature

At the core of this story is the question of what constitutes human nature. It especially emerges through the different characters' actions and personalities. While Shmuel and Bruno represent the childlike capacity for good and kindness, Lieutenant Kotler and Father demonstrate man's ability to execute unbelievable cruelty. In a story about the Holocaust, this question of how humans are inclined to treat one another and react in tragic situations is at the forefront.

Boyne seems to suggest that humans are constantly choosing how to treat themselves and others, rather than pointing to an inherent tendency for good or evil. Even at a young age, Bruno is able to change his perspective regarding live at "Out-With" throughout the course of the story. In contrast, Gretel chooses to become indoctrinated and wrapped up in the evil of the Nazi brainwashing.

Innocence

The theme of innocence is tied to that of Bruno's childlike misunderstanding of the tragedy through which he is living. His innocence prevents him from understanding, in the last chapters, the fate he is about to experience in the gas chamber. As he is marched along with the other prisoners, "he wanted to whisper to them that everything was all right, that Father was the Commandant, and if this was the kind of thing that he wanted the people to do then it must be all right" (210). Bruno is, of course, completely wrong: this is the sort of thing Father wants the Jews to do, but there is nothing "all right" about it. The very character in whom Bruno has faith is the one who is bringing about the deaths of so many, his own son included.

The Boy in the Striped Pajamas Quotes and Analysis

> *"What happened then was both unexpected and extremely unpleasant. Lieutenant Kotler grew very angry with Pavel and no one - not Bruno, not Gretl, not Mother and not even Father - stepped in to stop him doing what he did next, even though none of them could watch. Even though it made Bruno cry and Gretel grow pale."*
>
> *Narrator, 148-149*

This is a description of one of the only acts of violence Bruno witnesses during the story. Lieutenant Kotler, the young soldier whom Bruno has always disliked, attacks Pavel for spilling a bottle of wine into his lap as he tries to refill his glass. Boyne purposefully leaves out the details of the violent act, allowing it to represent the large-scale violence of the Holocaust itself and, by extension, of any genocide. In this interaction, Bruno and his family represent bystanders who are disgusted and disturbed by the violence but nevertheless do nothing to interfere with it or stop it.

> *"I'm thirteen years old, for heaven's sake! I can't afford to act like a child even if you can."*
>
> *Gretel, 159*

This is Gretel's response to Bruno when he asks her if she has her own imaginary friend. He has just lied to her about Shmuel, having accidentally let the boy's name slip. Despite Gretel's insistence that she is too mature to act like a child, when she leaves his room, Bruno hears her talking to her dolls. This tension between her perception of herself as a teenager versus her childlike behavior characterizes Gretel as representative of her peer group in Nazi-occupied Germany. If her family had stayed in Berlin, she ostensibly would have been a member of the Hitler Youth.

> *"Of course all this happened a long time ago and nothing like that could ever happen again. Not in this day and age."*
>
> *Narrator, 216*

Boyne issues a veiled call to action to the reader in the last statement of the story, after Father, devastated at having realized that his son has become the victim of his own concentration camp, is taken away from Auschwitz. Boyne means for the reader to consider just the opposite of this ironic comment: of course there *are* genocides occurring in this day and age, all over the world, and the reader is likely employing various coping strategies to ignore or dismiss them. This idea is a commentary on the perspective of those who allowed the Holocaust to occur while they remained removed from it, since it did not affect them personally. It applies to all witnesses to genocide in any time or place. The reader is meant to question how easy it is to watch "from a distance," as long as one is not victimized.

"Some people make all the decisions for us."

Mother, 14

Mother says this aloud as she opens a box to unpack at the family's new home near Auschwitz. Bruno knows that when Mother uses the phrase "some people," she means Father. This quotation is representative of Mother's passive-aggressive discontent at the family's situation, as well as of women's general lack of power.

"A home is not a building or a street or a city or something so artificial as bricks and mortar. A home is where one's family is, isn't that right?"

Father, 47

Father says this to Bruno as part of his explanation of why Bruno ought to stop being upset about the family's move to Auschwitz. It is a reasonable, relatable thing to say, and the reader might agree with Father about what makes a home. In allowing the reader to relate to this otherwise horrible character, Boyne invites us to see our own humanity in the actions of the Nazis.

"Those people... well, they're not people at all, Bruno."

Father, 53

When Bruno asks Father about the Jews he has seen living on the other side of the fence, Father urges him not to worry about them or try to understand them. In this quotation, he offers the explanation for how the Nazis were able to carry out such atrocities against the Jews: they convinced themselves that they were not people, and therefore were not entitled to basic human rights or even to life.

"I think I've always been here."

Pavel, 84

This is Pavel's answer to Bruno when the young boy asks him how long he has been at Auschwitz. Pavel used to work as a doctor and has been relegated to work as Bruno's family's cook and server. He has been stripped not only of his profession, but of his humanity, and his resignation to his fate is clear in this answer. Prisoners at Auschwitz lost track of time and often lost track of their sense of self.

"The people you have to dinner in this house. Why, it makes me sick. And to see you in that uniform makes me want to tear the eyes from my head!"

Grandmother, 93

This is Grandmother's reaction to the news that her son, Bruno's father, has been promoted by Adolf Hitler. She is referring to the evening in which The Fury and Eva had dinner with Bruno's parents, and isexpressing her disbelief and disapproval. Her character represents those Germans who did not support the rise of the Nazi party, but it also points to the powerlessness of women who might have had strong opinions. Their voices were not heard about the march toward world domination through genocide.

> *"It's so unfair. I don't see why I have to be stuck over here on this side of the fence where there's no one to talk to and no one to play with and you get to have dozens of friends and are probably playing for hours every day. I'll have to speak to Father about it."*
>
> *Bruno, 111*

In his first conversation with Shmuel, Bruno reveals how little he understands about the situation at Auschwitz. This quotation represents an instance of dramatic irony, in which the reader understands that Bruno has a backward conception of the way things are: while the situation is unfair, it is Shmuel who is "stuck" on the wrong side of the fence. This quotation represents Bruno's childlike misunderstanding of the Holocaust as well as his innocence at this point in the story.

> *"I'm very sorry, Shmuel...I can't believe I didn't tell him the truth. I've never let a friend down like that before. Shmuel, I'm ashamed of myself."*
>
> *Bruno, page 175*

This is Bruno's apology to Shmuel after he fails to speak up for his friend to Lieutenant Kotler. It is implied to the reader that his inaction resulted in physical harm to Shmuel, and here is compelled to take responsibility for the pain he has caused. This moment sets him apart from Father and the other Nazis, who are causing pain on a much larger scale but do not take responsibility for it.

The Boy in the Striped Pajamas Study Guide: Chapters One and Two Summary and Analysis

Summary

Bruno, a young boy living in Berlin during the Nazi regime, arrives home from school one day to find his family's maid, Maria, packing up his things. When he asks his mother what is going on, she takes him downstairs and explains to him that they're going to move away. She frames it positively, saying that "it's going to be a great adventure" (3). Mother explains that Bruno's father's job is the reason they are all leaving their home in Berlin; someone Bruno knows only as "the Fury" has plans for his father's career. Bruno isn't quite sure what his father's job is; the jobs of his school-friends' fathers are much clearer to him.

When he asks his mother how far away they will be moving, she tells him it's quite far away and that he will have to say goodbye to his school friends, Karl, Daniel, and Martin. Bruno is unhappy with this news but when he complains, Mother silences him. She says she wishes they had more time to prepare, but "thanks to some people," they are leaving rather last-minute. Bruno knows that when his mother says, "some people," she's referring to Father.

Bruno thinks about how much he will miss his house in Berlin, especially the banister that he often slides down. He will also miss Grandfather and Grandmother, who currently live close by to Bruno's family. Bruno walks upstairs, resigned to help Maria pack his things, but briefly looks down to Father's office. He has been told and understands that Father's office is "Out Of Bounds At All Times And No Exceptions." He witnesses an argument between Mother and Father, which father apparently wins, but Bruno can't make out the words.

Chapter Two begins with a comparison of Bruno's old home in Berlin to his new living situation. His old home in Berlin was very large and spacious, with beautiful furniture and decorations, as well as many places for him to hide in and explore. Berlin itself was a bustling city with many stimulating sights and smells. He used to walk home from school with his friends Karl, Daniel, and Martin. They would pass people sitting at tables outside, eating and laughing.

In contrast, "there was something about the new house that made Bruno think that no one ever laughed there; that there was nothing to laugh at and nothing to be happy about" (13). They have brought Maria with them, and have taken on three new servants and an old man who prepares their dinner and waits on them during meals. This man is Pavel, though Bruno does not know his name yet. He does notice that the three servants and Pavel are "quite skinny and only ever [speak] to each other in whispering voices," which implies to the reader that they are prisoners at Auschwitz (13).

Bruno tells Mother that he thinks it was a bad idea to move there, but she tells him they must make the best of it. She says that they "don't have the luxury of thinking... Some people make all the decisions for us," referring to Father (13-14). Bruno encourages her to tell Father that she has changed her mind about moving there and that they should stop unpacking so they can move back to Berlin the very next day. She snaps at him and tells him to go help Maria unpack his things before marching away.

Bruno goes upstairs to help Maria unpack in his new bedroom, which he finds quite depressing. He asks the maid what she thinks of the situation, but she responds that she has nothing to say about it. Bruno starts complaining about Father's job but stops abruptly when a figure appears by his door. It is Lieutenant Kotler, a young man who will be working under Father. Bruno has a bad feeling about him. Bruno becomes even more depressed as he realizes that there will likely be nobody with whom to play in this new place. He crosses the room to look out his bedroom window, hoping to see Berlin. Instead, he sees something that makes him "feel very cold and unsafe" (20).

Analysis

Boyne concerns himself with the plight of female characters, though the details of their specific situations are revealed through the lens of Bruno's narration. In the first chapter, the reader recognizes that Father has power over Mother not only because his job is dictating where they move without her having a say in the matter, but because he actually silences her voice in the argument Bruno witnesses between them: "he heard her speaking loudly to [Father] until Father spoke louder than Mother could and that put a stop to their conversation" (10). This literal silencing of Mother is representative of the figurative silencing of women's voices at this point in history, as well as in many times of war.

Mother reacts passive-aggressively, the only way she can, for example by referring to Father as "some people." Bruno knows that "'some people' was a grown-up's word for 'Father' and one that he wasn't supposed to use himself" (9). When Bruno complains that he doesn't thinking moving was a good idea after all, Mother tells him that they "don't have the luxury of thinking" because "[some] people make all the decisions for us" (13-14).

One of the ways Boyne establishes that the third-person narration is from Bruno's childish point of view is through the use of capitalization and misnaming of specific, recognizable names. For example, Bruno refers to his father's boss as "the Fury"; the reader must infer that this is actually "the Furor," or Adolf Hitler. Bruno understands that Father's office is "Out Of Bounds At All Times And No Exceptions," a phrase that he has presumably memorized after hearing it many times from his parents. This way of thinking about things so concretely, of making sense of a rule and applying it to all situations, is a characteristic of Bruno that identifies him as a child.

Another way that Bruno's point of view is conveyed to the reader is through the use of specific similes to describe his feelings and reactions. For example, when Mother tells him that he must say goodbye to his school friends, he questions her, "spluttering out the words as if his mouth was full of biscuits that he'd munched into tiny pieces but not actually swallowed yet" (7). This imagery makes sense to the reader but very distinctly refers to a situation to which a chid can easily relate.

Because of the limits of the narrator, the reader is able to approach the horrors of the Holocaust as if he or she has no prior knowledge - much like Bruno. The reader is required to put together details Bruno notices in order to make sense of the larger issues at play. For example, in Chapter One, Bruno notices that Mother "couldn't have applied her make-up correctly that morning because the rims of her eyes were more red than usual, like his own after he'd been causing chaos and got into trouble and ended up crying" (3). Bruno cannot fathom that his mother has been crying, but this description reveals to the reader the extent of her sorrow and frustration.

The limited narrator also allows for much dramatic irony. For example, when Bruno describes his visceral reaction to the depressing new living situation which Father's job has brought them, the reader cannot help but compare his relatively comfortable situation to that of the imprisoned Jews, just on the other side of the fence. This dramatic irony is employed alongside purposefully-omitted information to encourage the reader to draw his or her own conclusions. For example, Chapter Two leaves the reader hanging, so to speak, by neglecting to describe what Bruno sees out his bedroom window beyond the fact that it makes Bruno "feel very cold and unsafe" (20). Since the reader likely has some prior knowledge of the Holocaust, they might guess that the scene Bruno witnesses has to do with the prisoners at Auschwitz, though Bruno cannot make sense of what he sees.

The Boy in the Striped Pajamas Study Guide: Chapters Three and Four Summary and Analysis

Summary

Chapter Three introduces Gretel, Bruno's older sister, whom he refers to as "Trouble From Day One" (21). She is three years older than Bruno and he is slightly scared of her and her friends, who often say nasty things to him. He realizes that one positive thing about not living in Berlin anymore is that her friends are not around to bully him for being the smallest boy in his class. He comforts himself with the idea that when they return to their home in Berlin, he might be big enough that they won't make fun of him anymore.

Bruno runs into Gretel's room and discovers her arranging her dolls around her room. She has brought her extensive doll collection with her from Berlin to their new home. She tells him she brought them because Father had said they would be at their new home "for the foreseeable future." Bruno doesn't understand what that phrase means and they agree that it must mean "weeks from now" (24). Gretel agrees with Bruno that their new living situation is horrible. She tells him that the place is called "Out-With," and explains that the man who had done Father's job previously had had to leave very quickly.

Bruno tells her that the other children don't look very friendly to him. When she asks him what other children he is talking about, he stalls before telling her what he means. First, he walks over to the window in her bedroom casually, and realizes that her view is of the driveway and a forest beyond it. He indicates that she should follow him into his room, and she does. He tells her that the children are outside his own window, and she hesitates before approaching it to look out. When she does, she sees what Bruno saw at the end of the previous chapter.

Chapter Four begins with a description of the view from Bruno's window. There are boys, men, and elderly men living together without women of any kind. Gretel wonders where the women are. Directly beneath Bruno's window is a garden with flowers; beyond that is a paved area with a bench; beyond that is a wire fence that extends farther than they can see. On the other side of the fence there is no grass or greenery, only low huts and smoke stacks in the distance.

Unable to make sense of what she is seeing, Gretel assumes, "This must be the countryside" (33). She has learned about the countryside, with its farmers and animals, in school. She wonders out loud whether this is their holiday home. Bruno disagrees, pointing out that if it were a farm, there would be animals around, and there don't appear to be. The dirt ground also doesn't look as if it is capable of growing any food. Bruno wishes that Gretel would come up with an explanation and comfort him, but she doesn't.

Instead, Gretel wonders who the people are and what they're doing there. The boys and men are standing around, some working, some being intimidated by soldiers, some just staring at the ground "as if it was the sort of game where they didn't want to be spotted" (36). There seem to be hundreds of people, with huts extending into the distance. Gretel wonders why they would have moved here, to "such a nasty place and with so many neighbors" (37).

Bruno witnesses a group of boys huddled together, cowering from a group of soldiers. Bruno points out to Gretel that he was right about there being children, but Gretel says they look filthy and that she wouldn't want to play with them. She says she is going back to her room, where the view from the window is much nicer, and leaves Bruno alone. Bruno continues to watch the people out his bedroom window and notices that they're all wearing the same thing: "a pair of grey striped pajamas with a grey striped cap on their heads" (38).

Analysis

Boyne uses the technique of withholding information from the reader to build tension. At the end of Chapter Two, Bruno looked out his window and saw something, though the reader was not told what that was. In Chapter Three, he tells Gretel that he saw other children out his window, and she looks out herself to see them. But the reader is still denied a description of exactly what the scene is outside Bruno's window. In Chapter Four, the reader is finally provided with a description of the concentration camp.

Boyne continues to use capitalization and misnaming of recognizable things to establish Bruno's point of view in these chapters. Bruno's sister, Gretel, is described as being "Trouble From Day One" (21). In Chapter Three, Gretel tells Bruno that the place they are now living is called "Out-With," and this is what he continues to call it from this point on in the story. It is clearly a misunderstanding of the name "Auschwitz," but by refusing to name the concentration camp, Boyne avoids specificity to a certain extent. This allows the fable a sense of timelessness, extending beyond the specific situation at Auschwitz.

Gretel's character is dynamic throughout the story. When we first meet her in Chapter Three, she is clearly a child, though a few years older than Bruno. She spends most of her time arranging her dolls and has brought the entire collection from Berlin with her. Significantly, she is the one who tells Bruno that the name of their new home is "Out-With." This misnaming of the specific location marks Gretel as a child at this point, in contrast to the teenager she will grow into by the end of the story.

In the conversation between Bruno and Gretel, both naive children at this point in the story, Boyne creates dramatic irony. Bruno and Gretel do not know where they are, nor do they understand the concept of the war or of a concentration camp. But the 21st-century reader is meant to pick up on hints in order to put together what is actually going on. For example, when Bruno watches the people in the concentration camp outside his bedroom window, he notices that "a few stood near the huts in quiet groups, staring at the ground as if it was the sort of game where they didn't want to be spotted" (36). Of course, they do not want to be spotted by the Nazi soldiers, for fear of death. But Bruno can only make sense of this a kind of game that he might play himself.

In contrast to the technique of dramatic irony, Boyne sometimes encourages the reader to see the world of the story through Bruno's perspective. For example, when Gretel looks out the window and sees that he was telling the truth about the people outside, Bruno feels "quietly pleased with himself because whatever it was that was out there - and whoever *they* were - he had seen it first and he could see it whenever he wanted because they were outside his bedroom window and not hers and therefore they belonged to him and he was the king of everything they surveyed and she was his lowly subject" (32). The lack of punctuation creates a child-like "stream of consciousness" narration, leading to the hyperbolic conclusion that Bruno is the king and Gretel is his subject.

The Boy in the Striped Pajamas Study Guide: Chapters Five and Six Summary and Analysis

Summary

Bruno decides to speak to Father, who arrived at Out-With a few days earlier. Bruno remembers leaving their house in Berlin that morning - it hadn't looked like their home anymore, with all the furniture and decorations packed up. Before they left, Mother had said, "We should never have let the Fury come to dinner... Some people and their determination to get ahead" (40). Maria had overheard her and Mother had tried to backtrack, becoming embarrassed. Maria had been embarrassed, too, and had quickly gotten in the car.

After leaving their house in Berlin, Bruno and his family had arrived at the train station. On the other side of the train tracks from their train, there had been another train being boarded by crowds of people looking uncomfortable. It occured to Bruno that since the trains are going in the same direction, some of them might come on board his train, but he doesn't say anything.

Now, at Out-With, Bruno watches his Father standing in a circle of men outside his new home office. Bruno overhears them talking poorly of the former commandant. Father silences them and reminds them that they will have a new beginning tomorrow, with him as their leader. As they leave, they salute him and shout out "the two words that Bruno had been taught to say whenever anyone said it to him" (44). Bruno approaches Father's office cautiously, since he has been told it is Out Of Bounds At All Times And No Exceptions. He knocks and Father tells him to come in.

Father's office seems to Bruno to be much better decorated and more welcoming than the rest of the new house. Father is friendly but gruff toward Bruno, asking him how unpacking is going and if he has been helping Mother and Maria. Bruno is honest with him and tells him he does not like their new home. When Bruno asks when they can return to Berlin, Father tells him to give Out-With a chance, because it is their home now, "for the foreseeable future" (48). Bruno points out that Grandfather and Grandmother are not with them, nor are his school friends, but Father insists that this is one of those things in life that they don't have a choice in.

Father tells him that he remembers being a boy and wanting to disobey his own father, but he now realizes how foolish he was. He asks Bruno, "Do you think that I would have made such a success of my life if I hadn't learned when to argue and when to keep my mouth shut and follow orders?" (49). Bruno asks him if he has upset the Fury somehow, and if being moved to Out-With is a punishment. Father assures him it is just the opposite, that this is an important position. Father runs out of patience and tells Bruno that he has been treating him kindly during this conversation, but now it is over. Bruno bursts into tears, surprising himself, and Father tells him to go to his room.

Before he leaves, Bruno asks Father who the people are outside his window. His father thinks he is talking about the staff and the soldiers. But Bruno clarifies that he is referring to the people dressed the same, on the other side of the fence. Father answers that "[those people]... well, they're not people at all, Bruno... at least not as we understand the term" (53). He tells Bruno not to worry, since Bruno "[has] nothing whatsoever in common with them" (*ibid.*). Bruno leaves, accidentally forgetting to salute. When his father reminds him, he snaps his heels together and salutes, saying, "Heil Hitler," which he assumes is just a pleasant way to say goodbye.

A few days later, Bruno lies on his bed staring at the cracks in the ceiling. Maria enters his room and begins to put away his folded laundry. He engages her in conversation, hoping she will agree with him that Out-With is a horrible place, but she avoids saying anything negative. Bruno thoughtlessly says, "Stupid Father," which causes Maria to recoil in horror (59). She tells him that his father is a good man: her own mother worked as a dressmaker for Bruno's Grandmother. Bruno's Father paid for Maria's mother's hospital care and funeral when she became ill and eventually died, and then offered Maria and home, food, and a job in his household. She hints that she cannot understand how such a good man could be doing Father's job at Out-With, without actually saying those words.

Gretel barges in, startling Maria, and demands that Maria run her bath. Bruno sticks up for Maria, saying Gretel can run her own bath, but Maria obeys Gretel anyway. When Gretel storms off, telling Maria to hurry up, Bruno reiterates that he thinks Father has made a mistake taking the whole family to a new home. Maria insists that he stop speaking up about it, imploring him, "Don't you know how much trouble you could cause? For all of us?" (65). Bruno is unnerved by her expression of frantic worry and feels the urge to cry. He runs outside the house.

Analysis

The tension of being a woman without much power to control one's own life arises in Chapter Five with the character of Mother. Unaware that Maria can hear her, she speaks badly about her husband's ambition at the price of his family's comfort. When she realizes that Maria has overheard her, she stutters and tries to explain herself, clearly embarrassed that she has been caught criticizing her husband's decision. Just like so many women during times of war throughout history, Mother is swept up in events that are out of her control and does not feel she has a voice to defend herself or her family.

The theme of unnaturalness, especially as it relates to Auschwitz and the Holocaust generally, is introduced in Chapter Six. Instead of answering Bruno's question about whether she likes it at Out-With, Maria describes how much she loved the garden at the house in Berlin: "Sometimes, when it was a warm afternoon, I liked to sit out there in the sunshine and eat my lunch underneath the ivy tree by the pond. The flowers were very beautiful there. The scents. The way the bees hovered around and never bothered you if you just left them alone" (58). Bruno takes this as an indirect answer to his question, since it contrasts so starkly with the atmosphere at Auschwitz.

Boyne continues the technique of omitting information in order to encourage the reader to take on Bruno's point of view. As the soldiers leave Father's office in Chapter Five, they salute him and shout out "the two words that Bruno had been taught to say whenever anyone said it to him" (44). The reader might know that those two words are likely, "Heil Hitler!"; but, by leaving that specific information out, Boyne creates a sense of timelessness. These are Nazi soldiers at Auschwitz, but they could just as easily be soldiers obeying orders in any other genocide during human history or in the future.

Boyne embeds questions and key ideas about the nature of human interaction into the characters' conversations in order to draw the reader's attention to larger issues. For example, Father asks Bruno, "Do you think that I would have made such a success of my life if I hadn't learned when to argue and when to keep my mouth shut and follow orders?" (49). With this question, he summarizes the mentality of so many Nazi soldiers and German citizens during World War II. He is not a sympathetic character, but Boyne gives him some depth in order to offer an explanation for how such atrocities could have come to take place. Further, he assures Bruno that the Jews on the other side of the fence are "not people at all" - this is how he justifies to himself killing them at Auschwitz (53).

Maria's conversation with Bruno in Chapter Six serves not only to develop her back story, but to deepen the character of Father. She tells Bruno that his father gave her a job, a home, and food to eat, paid for her mother's hospital care and funeral. She serves as a commentary on the mental and emotional disconnect for Nazi soldiers generally, who might do kind deeds and appear to be wonderful people in other parts of their lives but also exterminate Jews. She tells Bruno that his father "has a lot of kindness in his soul, truly he does, which makes me wonder... Wonder what he... how he can..." (62). With this statement, Maria emerges as the first character who seems to have a moral conflict with the genocide taking place on the other side of the fence. Even so, because of her class restrictions and dependence on Father for a living, she tells Bruno to stop complaining.

Bruno's conversations with Father and Maria in Chapters Five and Six, respectively, introduce the adults' own fears about what they cannot control. For most of their conversation, Father has been patiently humoring Bruno. But when Bruno suggests that he should "apologize to the Fury" for whatever he has done that has landed them at Out-With, Father loses patience (50). When Maria tells Bruno to stop talking about how much he hates Out-With, she asks, "Don't you know how much trouble you could cause? For all of us?" (65). This question implies that if they are seen as not complying with the mission of the Nazi party, especially the extermination of the

Jews, they could be punished as swiftly and severely as the previous commandant, whose position Father now holds.

The childlike voice of the third-person narration continues in Chapters Five and Six as more details are revealed to the reader about Bruno's family's situation and whereabouts. Bruno understands that certain things are Out Of Bounds At All Times And No Exceptions; his father's office, for example. Later, he will be told that the other side of the fence at Out-With also falls into this category. When Father prompts him shout "Heil Hitler!" upon leaving the office at the end of Chapter Five, Bruno assumes this notorious Nazi salute is just "another way of saying, 'Well, goodbye for now, have a pleasant afternoon'" (54).

The Boy in the Striped Pajamas Study Guide: Chapters Seven, Eight, and Nine Summary and Analysis

Summary

Several weeks go by and Bruno begins to worry that if he doesn't find some way to entertain himself at Out-With, he will go crazy. He remembers that a mad man lived on the same street as his family in Berlin, Herr Roller. When Bruno made fun of him, Mother had scolded him, saying that Herr Roller had suffered a head injury when he served with Father during the Great War. Before his injury, he had been lively and loved to dance. Bruno decides that in order to have some fun, he will build himself a rope swing on the oak tree outside the house.

Bruno goes outside to find Gretel flirting with Lieutenant Kotler. Neither of his parents are home, and he is uncomfortable watching his sister talk to this solder, about whom Bruno has a bad feeling. Bruno asks about a spare tire, and Lieutenant Kotler makes a joke that goes over his head. When Gretel laughs, Bruno reminds her that she is only twelve years old and is herself a child. This greatly upsets her, since she wants to appear mature to Lieutenant Kotler. When Bruno explains that he wants the spare tire to make a rope swing, Lieutenant Kotler says he remembers having a rope swing when he was a boy. He yells rudely to Pavel, who is nearby, telling him to go to the storage shed with Bruno to retrieve a spare tire there. Bruno follows Pavel, reluctantly leaving Gretel alone with Lieutenant Kotler, whom he does not trust.

Bruno constructs the swing and, a couple of hours later, falls off of it. He injures himself, scraping up his knee pretty badly. Pavel, who has seen the whole thing from inside the kitchen where he has been peeling vegetables, runs out to help Bruno. Since Mother is still not home, Pavel cleans Bruno's wounds in the kitchen. He tells Bruno that he used to be a doctor, which confuses Bruno, since he has always just known Pavel as the person who prepares the family's vegetables and waits on them during dinner. Bruno tells Pavel that he wants to grow up to be an explorer. When Mother returns home, Pavel goes back to peeling the vegetables. Mother tells Bruno to go to his room and he overhears her saying to Pavel, "If the Commandant Asks, we'll say that I cleaned Bruno up" (85).

More than anyone else from Berlin, Bruno misses his Grandfather and Grandmother. His Grandfather had run a restaurant in the town center, and his Grandmother had been a famous singer. She could always be talked into performing for the guests at a party and would organize plays for Bruno and Gretel to perform with her, costumes and all. Bruno remembers the last play they had put on, about a week after Father's promotion to Commandant, had ended in a dramatic argument. It had been Christmas Day, and Father had decided to wear his new uniform.

After dinner and the production, Grandmother, the only one who disapproved of Father's new uniform, had said to her son, "I wonder if all the performances I made you give as a boy led you to this. Dressing up like a puppet on a string" (90). Grandfather had encouraged her to be quiet, but she had not obeyed. Mother had tried to calm her down by asking her to confirm that Father looks handsome in his new uniform, but Grandmother was incredulous at the suggestion that how he looks would be important. Mother had told Gretel and Bruno to go upstairs, but they eavesdropped from the top of the stairs. When Father called himself a patriot, Grandmother had yelled, "A patriot indeed! The people you have to dinner in this house. Why, it makes me sick. And to see you in that uniform makes me want to tear the eyes from my head!" (93). She had stormed out of their house, and Bruno hadn't seen her since. He decides to write her a letter from Out-With, telling her how unhappy he is in their new home and how much he misses her.

More time passes at Out-With. One day, Father decides to hire a man named Herr Liszt as a tutor for Gretel and Bruno. Herr Liszt focuses on history and geography, neither of which is very interesting to Bruno, but the tutor insists that he learn about "The Fatherland" (98). He disapproves of Bruno's creative mind and wants instead to teach him "about the great wrongs that have been done to you" (98). Bruno assumes Herr Liszt is referring to how Bruno has been forced to come live at Out-With, so he agrees.

A few days later, Bruno gets the urge to go exploring, something he used to love to do before coming to Out-With. He has been watching the people on the other side of the fence from his bedroom window, wondering why they were so different from him. Although he sometimes sees the soldiers on that side of the fence, he never sees the people in the striped pajamas on his side of it. So Bruno ventures out and decides to walk along the fence as far as he can. Before he heads off, though, he examines the bench on the pavement outside his house. There is a plaque on it that marks it as having been presented on the opening of Out-With, in June of 1940. Then he begins to walk along the fence, although Mother and Father have told him many times that exploration is banned at Out-With.

Analysis

Boyne continues to use the technique of omitting specific information in Chapter Seven. In this case, it is the derogatory term that Lieutenant Kotler calls Pavel, which Bruno doesn't understand: "'Hey, you!' he shouted, then adding a word that Bruno did not understand. 'Come over here, you--' He said the word again, and something about the harsh sound of it made Bruno look away and feel ashamed to be part of this at all'" (75). By not specifically naming the word, Boyne both allows the reader to take on Bruno's childlike perspective and suggests the universality of this interaction.

Lieutenant Kotler could be any soldier during any war time, shouting a derogatory term to dehumanize a victim of any genocide.

Dramatic irony is in play in Chapters Eight and Nine, such as is seen during Bruno's conversation with Pavel in the kitchen. Bruno cannot understand what the reader knows: Pavel is a prisoner at Auschwitz, who has been torn away from his life as a practicing doctor and is being forced to wait on Bruno's family in the house. This dramatic irony is emphasized by the sentence fragment that makes up an entire paragraph following Pavel's description of all the things he used to do: "But not any more" (83). This suggests that Bruno understands Pavel's words carry some weight, but unlike the reader, he cannot make sense of the situation. In Chapter Nine, Bruno wonders about the people in the striped pajamas on the other side of the fence. He thinks about how "the pajama people all jumped to attention whenever the soldiers approached and sometimes they fell to the ground and sometimes they didn't even get up and had to be carried away instead" (101). To the reader, it is clear that the soldiers are killing the Jews during these interactions, but Bruno cannot comprehend that.

The dramatic irony of the situation around Bruno's rope swing injury is complemented by the limited third-person narration. Bruno is happy to hear Mother thank Pavel, "because surely it was obvious to everyone that if it hadn't been for him, he would have bled to death" (85). But of course, the opposite is true: Bruno, the child, is the person to whom this is obvious. Mother is grateful, but what she says next indicates that she knows Father would be furious if he heard that Pavel had touched Bruno, his son. So she demonstrates empathy and protects Pavel by saying she will cover for him if the Commandant asks who cleaned Bruno up. Bruno completely misinterprets this action, thinking it is selfish and "a way for Mother to take credit for something she hadn't done" (85).

The character of Herr Roller is introduced in Chapter Seven and doesn't appear again in the story. He is introduced through the technique of flashback, in which Bruno remembers a conversation he had with Mother regarding the man. Herr Roller's head injury and subsequent loss of mental facilities demonstrate an example of one of the costs of war. He is also an ex-German soldier who is a sympathetic character; his loss draws the reader's attention to the humanity of the German soldiers, even as they commit despicable acts against the Jews in WWII.

Gretel's character development into an indoctrinated follower of the Nazi party is introduced in Chapter Seven, when Bruno points out how young she is in front of Lieutenant Kotler. She responds by snapping at him, "her laughter stopped now, her face frozen in horror, 'I'll be thirteen in a couple of weeks' time. A teenager. Just like you'" (74). Her words to Lieutenant Kotler accomplish two things: first, they foreshadow her mental shift as she grows out of childhood; and second, they remind the reader that some of the Nazi soldiers committing horrible actions against the Jews in the concentration camps were indoctrinated teenagers.

The issue of gender inequality arises in the character of Grandmother in Chapter Eight. She is outspoken about her strong disapproval of Father's new appointment to

Commandant. When Grandfather tries to hush her, telling her they'd spoken about this before, she shoots back, "*You* discussed it, Mattias. I was merely the blank wall to whom you addressed your words. As usual" (91). This comment reveals that the inequality in their conversations mirrors that of the conversations between Mother and Father. Grandmother also represents the strongest voice among the female characters, who are the only ones with reservations about what is going on in their country. Maria must keep her silence because of her financial dependence on Bruno's Father and Mother makes small defiant gestures like protecting Pavel, but Grandmother spoke up about her disapproval. Unfortunately, because of her position as a woman, she is unable to do anything to stop her son from pursuing his career in the Nazi party.

The Boy in the Striped Pajamas Study Guide: Chapters Ten, Eleven, and Twelve Summary and Analysis

Summary

Bruno walks along the fence for about an hour without seeing anyone. Just as he starts feeling hungry and begins to think about turning back, he sees a tiny speck in the distance that, as he gets closer, turns out to be a little boy on the other side of the fence. Bruno approaches him and says hello. The boy is wearing the striped pajamas that all people on the other side of the fence wear, and on his upper arm is a band with the Star of David on it. Bruno doesn't know what the star is, but he notes the symbol. Bruno is "sure that he had never seen a skinnier or sadder boy in his life" (107).

Bruno strikes up a conversation with the boy, sitting down on his own side of the fence so he can talk with the boy through it. The boy tells him that his name is Shmuel; Bruno has never heard of that name, and Shmuel has never heard of Bruno's name. The boys discover that they are both nine years old and that, in fact, they were both born on April 15, 1934. Bruno asks if Shmuel has any friends on that side of the fence, and Shmuel tells him that there are many boys their age living there with him. Bruno tells Shmuel that he is from Berlin; Shmuel is from Poland, but he speaks German because his mother is a teacher - she speaks French, Italian, and English, too. Bruno tells Shmuel that "Germany is the greatest of all countries... We're superior" (112), but even as he says this, he realizes that his words sound rude. Shmuel reveals that they are currently *in* Poland, which comes as a surprise to Bruno, who doesn't quite know where Poland is. Bruno tells Shmuel about Berlin and how it has become noisy and scary recently, and Bruno tells him that where he comes from is probably nicer than Berlin.

Chapter Eleven takes the form of a flashback to a few months earlier, when Bruno's family still lived in Berlin. One night, Father had arrived home and informed the family that the Fury was coming to dinner. Mother had cleaned the house frantically to prepare. Father had prepared Bruno and Gretel for the Fury's arrival by telling them, "it is very important for my career that tonight goes well" (119). When the Fury had arrived, he was with a woman named Eva. In contrast to the Fury's brusque hostility - he was "the rudest guest Bruno had ever witnessed" - Eva had been kind to the children and had smiled at Bruno before the Father closed the door to the dining room (122). After the Fury and Eva had left, Bruno had overheard his parents' conversation about leaving Berlin. Days later, he had arrived home from school to find Maria packing his belongings.

Chapter Twelve returns to Bruno and Shmuel's conversation from opposite sides of the fence. Chapter Ten had ended with Bruno's question to Shmuel: "Why are there so many people on that side of the fence? And what are you all doing there?" (115). Shmuel answers by explaining his experience. He lived with his mother, father, and his brother Josef in an apartment above his father's watchmaking store. One day, his mother was making armbands for the family with the Star of David on them, and she told him he had to wear his whenever he left the house. Bruno tells Shmuel that his father wears an armband, too - only Father's armband has the Nazi symbol on it, while Shmuel's family's armbands have the Star of David.

Shmuel goes on to tell Bruno about how he came to live at Out-With. His family was told they had to move to a different part of Cracow, all cramped in one room with another family. They were on the wrong side of a wall that the soldiers had built. Bruno doesn't believe that so many people could have lived in only one room, but he doesn't tell Shmuel that. There were eleven people total living in that room, including one of the sons from the other family, Luka, who Shmuel tells Bruno "kept hitting me even when I did nothing wrong" (129). Bruno relates that Gretel sometimes hits him, too, but Shmuel doesn't respond to his observation.

Shmuel tells Bruno that one day soldiers arrived and packed him and everyone living nearby into huge trucks. Lots of people hid from the soldiers, but Shmuel believes they were all eventually found. They were brought to a train, which Shmuel says "was horrible... there was no air to breathe. And it smelled awful" (129). Bruno tells him that he should have gotten on the train Bruno took, the one on the other side of the platform, but Shmuel says his train had no doors. Bruno doesn't believe him about that detail, either. Shmuel tells him that when they got off the train, they all had to walk to Out-With; Bruno counters that his family "had a car" (130). He cannot understand why Shmuel seems so sad, since "after all much the same thing had happened to him" (130).

Shmuel tells Bruno that there are hundreds of other boys on his side of the fence, and Bruno reiterates his feeling that it is unfair for him to have no one to play with on *his* side. Shmuel tells him they don't play, and this surprises Bruno. Shmuel asks Bruno if he has any food and Bruno tells him that he had meant to bring chocolate, but forgot. Bruno tells him that dinner isn't served until half-past six, and invites Shmuel to come have dinner with his family sometime. When Shmuel doesn't return the invitation, Bruno suggests that perhaps he could come under the fence to visit with Shmuel and his friends. Shmuel becomes nervous and tells Bruno he has to go back because he'll be in trouble if they catch him. Bruno shouts after him that he'll be back tomorrow, and sets off for home. He decides to keep his new friend a secret from his family, since he doesn't want to be told he can't see Shmuel anymore.

Analysis

In Chapter Ten, Boyne sprinkles a bit of ironic humor into a story about horrific subject matter. When Bruno first sees Shmuel in the distance, he wonders about what kind of discovery this boy will be. Since he fancies himself an explorer, he considers that famous historical explorers never know what they will find: "[most] of the time they came across something interesting that was just sitting there, minding its own business, waiting to be discovered (such as America)" (105). This aside serves as a little joke to the reader, who is expected to know that America was, of course, *not* just waiting to be discovered by Europeans. There were entire advanced civilizations of people living there before the explorers Bruno has read about arrived. But as a child growing up in a German school system in the middle of the twentieth century, Bruno's understanding of American history is quite limited.

Shmuel, who is introduced in these chapters, serves as a mirror character for Bruno. Upon discovering that they were born on the same day, Bruno says "[we're] like twins" (110). The reader only learns about Shmuel through Bruno's perception of him and through what he tells Bruno about his life before arriving at Out-With. Boyne gives the two characters many similarities: they are both small for their age, they share a birthday, and they are both at Out-With. In Chapter Twelve, Shmuel describes how he came to have to wear his Star of David armband and draws the symbol in the dirt. Bruno points out that his Father wears one, too, and draws the Nazi symbol in the dirt on his side of the fence. They were both forced to leave their comfortable homes against their will. When Shmuel describes how he and his family were forced to come on a train to Out-With, Bruno cannot understand why Shmuel seems so sad, since "much the same thing had happened to him" (130).

But the key difference between them - that Shmuel is Jewish and thus a member of the oppressed group in this genocide, while Bruno happens to be German and thus a member of the oppressing group - is clear. When Bruno tells Shmuel that Father also wears an armband, Shmuel observes, "Yes, but they're different, aren't they?" (127). In addition, their names mark them as different. Shmuel is a distinctively Jewish name and Bruno is has never heard it before; Shmuel tells him "there are dozens of Shmuels on this side of the fence. Hundreds probably" (109). This represents the insurmountable gulf between their life experiences, which is the result of an arbitrary difference.

The dramatic irony that has been at play throughout the novel so far comes to the forefront in Bruno's conversation with Shmuel. Neither boy completely understands the situation he is experiencing, but Shmuel has more knowledge than Bruno. He is living in the concentration camp and witnesses horrors every day. When he tells Bruno that there are many boys their age living there with him, Bruno declares that "[it's] so unfair...I don't see why I have to be stuck over here on this side of the fence where there's no one to talk to and no one to play with and you get to have dozens of friends and are probably playing for hours every day. I'll have to speak to Father about it" (111). Shmuel does not correct him, but of course Shmuel is not "playing" on the other side of the fence. The irony is extended through Bruno's proposed solution: Father, whom he wants to solve the problem for him, is in fact the perpetrator of the genocide taking place at Out-With.

In Chapter Eleven, the limited third-person narration is used in a flashback to reveal details about Bruno's family's situation. The person Bruno refers to as "the Fury" is clearly Adolf Hitler, or "the Furor," as Father and Mother would have referred to him. Though Father does his best to impress the Fury and impresses upon his children that they ought to do the same, Bruno judges him harshly as "a horrible man" (124). In the snippets of conversation that Bruno overhears between his parents after the Fury and Eva leave their home in Berlin, it is revealed that Father has no real choice in the matter of moving to Out-With. He tells Mother, "...no choice, at least not if we want to continue... what would happen is I would be taken away and treated like a..." (124). The specifics of the situation are omitted to leave the details open to the reader's interpretation. But the implication is that if Father refused the appointment, he himself would be incarcerated.

The theme of the Holocaust being unnatural arises again in Chapter Eleven, in a snippet of conversation Bruno overhears between his parents. Mother protests the move to Out-With by saying, "...as if it's the most natural thing in the world and it's not, it's just not..." (124). It's unclear whether she is talking about her family moving away from Berlin or the concentration camps themselves, but Boyne is drawing attention to the natural vs. unnatural dichotomy again. The Nazis used the argument that the Aryan race was "naturally" superior to all others, using the idea of natural dominance as justification in exterminating the Jewish population. But Boyne turns this assumption on its head, pointing out throughout the story just how "unnatural" the atmosphere and situation at Out-With really is.

The Boy in the Striped Pajamas Study Guide: Chapters Thirteen and Fourteen Summary and Analysis

Summary

Weeks pass and Bruno visits with his new friend Shmuel regularly. One day, Maria finds him in the kitchen taking bread and cheese to bring to Shmuel. Bruno asks her about Pavel, who had told him that he wasn't really a waiter but was actually a doctor. Maria confirms that Pavel had been a doctor "in another life" (137). Maria agrees to tell Bruno what she knows about Pavel's life before he came to Out-With, but makes him promise not to speak of it to anyone else. The reader doesn't learn what she tells Bruno.

Bruno arrives to meet Shmuel a bit later that day. Having learned about Pavel's life from Maria, Bruno asks Shmuel if he knows the old man, but Shmuel tells him he doesn't. Bruno tells Shmuel he wants to be a soldier when he grows up, a "good soldier" like Father, but Shmuel tells him there aren't any good soldiers (140). Shmuel tries to reveal more to Bruno, whispering, "You don't know what it's like here" (*ibid.*), but Bruno purposefully ignores the statement because it makes him feel awkward. When he brings up Lieutenant Kotler, Shmuel says he doesn't like talking about him.

When Bruno gets home, he finds out to his disappointment that Lieutenant Kotler is joining the family for dinner. Pavel waits on them, seeming to Bruno to be a bit weaker than usual. Bruno brings up that he hates learning about history and Father scolds him for it. Lieutenant Kotler offers that his father was a professor of literature at the university, but that he had left Germany for Switzerland in 1938. This information embarrasses Lieutenant Kotler and disturbs Father, who comments with suspicion, "Strange that he chose not to stay in the Fatherland" (146). Bruno is frightened by the tension but also enjoys Father speaking harshly to Lieutenant Kotler. At that moment, Pavel uncorks a new bottle of wine and accidentally spills it on Lieutenant Kotler because his hands are shaking. Lieutenant Kotler reacts very angrily and violently, although the details of his actions against Pavel are not revealed. Bruno goes to bed extremely upset about what happened to Pavel.

Several more weeks pass and Bruno continues to visit Shmuel when Herr Liszt leaves after their lesson. One afternoon, Shmuel has a black eye but refuses to talk about it. Every day, Bruno asks if he can come over to the other side of the fence to play with Shmuel, but Shmuel always says it's not a good idea. He tells Bruno that the "striped pajamas" are the uniform he and the other prisoners were given when they arrived at Out-With. Bruno's lack of awareness is evident in his suggestion that Shmuel should just choose to wear something else when he wakes up in the morning, but Shmuel doesn't explain to him why that would be impossible.

One day it is raining too hard for Bruno to go outside. He is lying on his bed reading when Gretel comes into his room, bored. He accidentally mentions Shmuel to her and quickly covers his mistake by telling her that he is referring to his imaginary friend. In order to sell his lie, he remembers a time when Grandmother had walked in on him while he was going to the bathroom and other embarrassing moments so that his face will turn red. It works, and Gretel begins to make fun of him for having an imaginary friend. Bruno takes the opportunity to talk about Shmuel, now that he has made sure Gretel believes the boy is imaginary.

Bruno tells Gretel about how all of Shmuel's friends with whom he used to play "disappeared without even saying goodbye to him" (158). He goes on and tells her that yesterday, Shmuel told him that his grandfather has been missing for days and that whenever he asks his father about it, his father begins to cry and hugs him. As he describes what Shmuel has told him to Gretel, Bruno begins to feel guilty for not comforting Shmuel when his friend was telling him these things. Instead, he had changed the subject because he had felt uncomfortable. He decides to apologize for his callousness when he sees Shmuel the next day.

Gretel advises Bruno to stop talking to his imaginary friend. She tells him it indicates he is going crazy, but he tells her he doesn't want to stop. Gretel reassures him she won't tell anyone about his imaginary friend, and teasingly tells him she has her own. When he asks her if she's telling the truth, she scoffs, "I can't afford to act like a child, even if you can" (159) and leaves the room. Bruno hears her talking to her dolls in her own room. He loses interest in his book and stares out the window at the rain, wondering about Shmuel.

Analysis

In Chapter Thirteen, Boyne uses the technique of omitting information. Just as Maria sits down with Bruno in the kitchen and says, "All right... This is as much as I know" (137), the scene ends and the reader picks back up with Bruno arriving to meet Shmuel later that day. This achieves a sense of vagueness around Pavel's life - he is representative of the many Jews who were torn from their professions and brought to concentration camps, so his story could be anyone's. Likewise, when Lieutenant Kotler attacks Pavel for accidentally spilling the wine on him, the details of the interaction are omitted. The narrator only states that "[what] happened then was both unexpected and extremely unpleasant. Lieutenant Kotler grew very angry with Pavel and no one - not Bruno, not Gretel, not Mother and not even Father - stepped in to stop him doing what he did next, even though none of them could watch" (148-49). This omission of detail makes the interaction representative of all acts of violence against Jews at the hands of Nazis -- and, in fact, against the oppressed group in any genocide throughout history. Bruno and his family represent the bystanders who were repulsed by the violence and did not try to stop it.

Boyne continues to use dramatic irony throughout Bruno's conversation with Shmuel in Chapter Thirteen. When Bruno tells Shmuel about how Pavel had cleaned his knee when he fell off the tire swing, Shmuel comments that "[the] soldiers don't normally like people getting better... It usually works the other way round" (139). Bruno doesn't know what his friend is talking about, but the reader knows that the soldiers are killing the Jews in the concentration camp. If any of the prisoners falls ill or is unable to work, he will be shot rather than brought to a hospital to recover.

In Bruno's conversation with Gretel in Chapter Fourteen, the dramatic irony is used to reveal details about Shmuel's life on the other side of the fence. He mentions that Shmuel used to have friends to play with at Out-With, but that "they disappeared without even saying goodbye to him" (158). This dramatic irony works on two levels: that of Shmuel's perception, since his feelings were hurt when his friends disappeared; and that of Bruno's perception, since he understands even less of the situation than Shmuel does. The reader knows that the boys Shmuel used to play with have been killed by the Nazis and that they would never have been given the opportunity to say goodbye to anyone. Further, Shmuel doesn't know where his grandfather has gone, but by Bruno's description to Gretel of what happens when Shmuel asks about it, it is clear to the reader that Shmuel's father does know: "whenever he asks his father about him he starts crying and hugs him so hard that he's worried he's going to squeeze him to death" (158). In recounting these details to Gretel, even though he doesn't understand the full extent of the horror that has taken place, Bruno realizes that he should have tried to comfort his friend.

The conversation at the dinner table in Chapter Thirteen reveals a bit more about the political climate in Germany leading up to the current moment of the story. Lieutenant Kotler reveals that his father, a professor of literature, left the country in 1938 to go to Switzerland. This upsets Father, who suspects Lieutenant Kotler's father had "disagreements" with the way the country was headed in 1938, lumping him in with the "traitors" and "cowards" who had left to avoid the Nazis (147). Lieutenant Kotler makes a point of distancing himself from his father in the Commandant's eyes, insisting that "[we're] not close, my father and I" (146).

The distinction between Bruno as a child and Gretel as a young teenager begins to develop in Chapter Fourteen. There is a still a connection between them as they talk on a rainy day while they are both bored. Bruno feels comfortable enough to tell Gretel about Shmuel's life, although he pretends Shmuel is an imaginary friend. When Bruno asks Gretel if she has an imaginary friend, she laughs at him and says, "No... I'm thirteen years old, for heaven's sake! I can't afford to act like a child even if you can" (159). However, when she leaves his room, he hears her talking to her dolls. This tension between her perception of herself as a teenager versus her childlike behavior characterizes Gretel as representative of her peer group in Nazi-occupied Germany. If her family had stayed in Berlin, she would have become a member of the Hitler Youth.

The Boy in the Striped Pajamas Study Guide: Chapters Fifteen, Sixteen, and Seventeen Summary and Analysis

Summary

The rain continues on and off for the next few weeks, during which Bruno is unable to meet with Shmuel as often as he would like. When he does see Shmuel, he notices that he is getting even thinner and more sickly looking, so Bruno tries to remember to bring him more food. Meanwhile, Mother is planning a birthday party for Father and Lieutenant Kotler is spending a lot of time at the house with her. This makes Bruno uncomfortable and he dislikes the young soldier even more that he already had, especially since Lieutenant Kotler is always joking with Mother and "Mother [laughs] at his jokes more than she [laughs] at Father's" (162).

On the day before Father's birthday party, Bruno runs into Lieutenant Kotler in the hallway and the soldier grabs Bruno's book, *Treasure Island*, from his hands. He taunts Bruno a bit before Mother enters, calling Lieutenant Kotler, "Kurt, precious" before realizing that Bruno is there (165). She sends Bruno into the kitchen, where he is surprised to find Shmuel sitting at the table. Lieutenant Kotler has brought him there because his hands are small enough to polish the glasses for Father's birthday party. Bruno begins to help himself to some cold chicken and stuffing that's in the refrigerator and when he sees Shmuel looking at the food, he offers his friend some. Shmuel is hesitant because he knows he'll get in trouble if Lieutenant Kotler returns, but Bruno puts the food in his hands and he scarfs it down.

Lieutenant Kotler returns and scolds Shmuel for not polishing the glasses. When he accuses Shmuel of stealing food to eat, Shmuel tells him that Bruno gave it to him, and that Bruno is his friend. But when Lieutenant Kotler asks Bruno if he knows the boy, Bruno denies it. Lieutenant Kotler tells Shmuel to finish polishing the glasses, and that when he brings him back to the camp, they "will have a discussion about what happens to boys who steal" (173). When Lieutenant Kotler tells Bruno to go read his book, Bruno obeys and leaves the kitchen, feeling incredibly guilty about having betrayed his friend.

For almost a week, Shmuel does not come back to meet him at the fence. When his friend finally returns, his face is covered in bruises. When Bruno asks about his injuries, Shmuel says it doesn't hurt anymore. Bruno apologizes for letting him down and says he's ashamed of himself. Shmuel smiles and forgives him, lifting up the fence so that they can shake hands beneath it. It is the first time the two boys have ever touched.

At this point, almost a year has passed since Bruno and his family left Berlin to come to Out-With. The family receives news that Grandmother has died, so they return to their old home in Berlin for two days to attend the funeral. The two days are so sad that Bruno is almost relieved to return to Out-With. In fact, he muses that things are pretty positive at his new home recently: Mother is no longer taking as many "afternoon naps or medicinal sherries" (178) and Gretel is staying out of Bruno's way for the most part. Additionally, Lieutenant Kotler has been suddenly transferred away from Out-With, coinciding with a huge fight between Mother and Father. Mostly, Bruno is happy because his friendship with Shmuel has become even stronger.

Bruno has begun to wonder more and more about why he and Shmuel are living on opposite sides of the fence, so he decides to ask Gretel about it. She has thrown away all of her dolls and replaced them with maps of Europe. When he asks her about the fence, she first corrects him on his pronunciation of "Out-With." Then she explains that the people on the other side of the fence are Jews and that the fence is there to keep them from getting out and mixing with anyone else. When Bruno asks her what he and their family are, if not Jews, she says simply that they are "the opposite" (183).

While they are talking, Gretel notices something in her hair and begins screaming. Mother arrives and finds that both Gretel and Bruno have lice. They treat their hair with a special shampoo, but then Father goes a step further and insists that Bruno have all his hair shaved off. Father shaves it off himself. When Bruno looks at himself in the mirror, he feels sick, but thinks that now he looks even more like Shmuel. When they see each other the next day, Shmuel laughs at Bruno.

For the next few weeks, Mother becomes more and more unhappy. Bruno overhears her speaking with Father in the office one day and learns that she wants to return to Berlin with Bruno and Gretel, leaving Father to work at Out-With by himself. Mother begins napping even more and having even more medicinal sherries, causing Bruno to worry about her health. Then Father calls Gretel and Bruno into his office and asks them if they miss Berlin. Gretel confirms that she does, but Bruno is hesitant because he knows he would miss Shmuel if they left. Father tells them that the Fury will not relieve him of his command, but that Mother wants to go back to Berlin immediately.

Father remarks that perhaps she is right that Out-With is "not a place for children" (191). Bruno pipes up that there are hundreds of children there, but they are living on the other side of the fence. Father is surprised that Bruno has noticed them, but this information seems to help him make the final decision that the children should return to Berlin with Mother. Preparations begin so that Mother, Gretel, and Bruno can return to Berlin that week, but Bruno is nervous about telling Shmuel the news.

Analysis

The limitations of the third-person narrator are apparent in describing the relationship between Lieutenant Kotler and Mother. Bruno is made uncomfortable by it, but he doesn't understand the extent of it. All he knows is that "whenever Father was called away to Berlin on an overnight trip the lieutenant hung around the house as if he were in charge: he would be there when Bruno was going to bed and be back again in the morning before he even woke up" (163). The reader is meant to understand that Mother and Lieutenant Kotler are having an affair, but that possibility doesn't even cross Bruno's mind. When Lieutenant Kotler is suddenly transferred away from Out-With in Chapter Sixteen, Bruno notes that "there had been a lot of shouting between Father and Mother about it late at night," but it doesn't occur to him that Father has discovered Mother's affair with the young soldier and sent Lieutenant Kotler away as a result (178).

Gretel's character develops further in Chapter Sixteen, and now she has firmly arrived on the other side of childhood. She has replaced her collection of dolls with maps of Europe given to her by Father, which she updates using the newspapers each day as she reads about developments in the war. Her transition out of childhood naivete is represented clearly in her correction of Bruno's mispronunciation of "Out-With." It was she who first told him the name of the place, but now she corrects him. When he asks her about the fence, she explains to him that their family is "the opposite" of the Jews on the other side of the fence (183). Her understanding of the situation is still simplistic and lacks understanding: she has accepted what her Father and Herr Liszt have taught her without much critical thinking.

The theme of the natural versus the unnatural emerges again in Chapter Fifteen, in the metaphor used to describe the differences between Bruno's and Shmuel's hands: "[although] Bruno was small for his age, and certainly not fat, his hand appeared healthy and full of life. The veins weren't visible through the skin, the fingers weren't little more than dying twigs" (168). Shmuel's living situation at Out-With is unnatural and thus, like a withering tree, he is slowly dying. The difference in the boys' hands is presented as a physical representation of just how different their life experiences are at Out-With. Shmuel tells Bruno that "[everyone] on my side of the fence looks like this now" (168).

Bruno's betrayal of Shmuel in front of Lieutenant Kotler is representative of the many people who betrayed their Jewish neighbors and friends during the Holocaust in similar ways. By distancing himself from Shmuel because he is afraid of the consequences of associating with the boy, Bruno contributes to Shmuel's punishment for a crime he did not commit: stealing food. The way Bruno considers his actions immediately following the event reflects a personal disconnect: "[he] wondered how a boy who thought he was a good person really could act in such a cowardly way toward a friend" (174). He feels ashamed of himself, but does not take action to right the wrong. When Shmuel finally returns to meet him at the fence, his face covered in bruises, Bruno apologizes. His words could have easily come from any of the

Germans who fell in line with the Nazis and didn't speak up for the Jews during the Holocaust.

Certain events in Chapters Fifteen and Sixteen foreshadow the tragic conclusion of the story. First, Shmuel lifts up the fence that separates the two boys so that they can shake hands beneath it. It is the first time they have touched, and it foreshadows the moment when Bruno will crawl under the fence to help Shmuel look for his father. In Chapter Sixteen, after discovering that he and Gretel both have lice, Bruno must have all his hair shaved off. He and Shmuel both think it makes them look even more alike. Significantly, it is Father who shaves all of Bruno's hair off, inadvertently making it possible for his son to be confused for a Jew when he crosses under the fence.

When Bruno overhears Mother confronting Father in Chapter Seventeen, the reader learns more about the power dynamic between his parents. In the previous chapter when her children got lice, Mother complained, "If some people could only see the effect this place is having on us all" (185). She had been passive-aggressively referring to Father, just as she always has throughout the story. But in Chapter Seventeen, she speaks up for herself and demands to leave Out-With. She tells Father, "This is *your* assignment, not ours. You stay if you want to" (187). At a time when gender roles determined that a wife obey her husband, this distinction between his responsibilities and her own is a bold statement.

The Boy in the Striped Pajamas Study Guide: Chapters Eighteen, Nineteen, and Twenty Summary and Analysis

Summary

Shmuel does not come to meet Bruno at the fence for the two days after Bruno finds out he will be returning to Berlin soon. On the third day, when Shmuel does appear, he is even sadder than usual. He tells Bruno that his father has disappeared. When Bruno suggests asking his own Father what has happened, Shmuel says he doesn't think that's a good idea because the soldiers hate him and the rest of the people on that side of the fence. He vehemently says that he hates the soldiers, too. When Bruno asks him if he hates Father, too, Shmuel says nothing but wonders how Bruno could be the son of such a hateful person.

Bruno tells Shmuel that he is returning to Berlin. Shmuel is saddened by this news, since he won't have anyone to talk to anymore. Bruno tells him that tomorrow will be the last time they'll see each other, and that he wishes they had gotten a chance to play together. Shmuel suggests that he come over to the other side of the fence, but Bruno reminds him that he would get in trouble. Then Bruno realizes that since he's had his head shaved, he looks a lot more like Shmuel. If Shmuel brings him a pair of striped pajamas, he will be able to sneak over to the other side of the fence secretly and he can help Shmuel search for his father. They make a plan to do it the next day, Friday. Bruno is excited about the chance to have an adventure with his friend and Shmuel is excited that Bruno is going to help him look for his father.

Bruno wakes up on Friday and is disappointed to see that it is raining. Just as Herr Liszt is leaving for the day, the rain begins to let up. Bruno puts on boots and a raincoat and walks through the mud to meet Shmuel at the fence. Shmuel says he had been unsure whether Bruno would come to meet him in the rain, but he has brought with him a pair of dirty-looking striped pajamas. He hands the pajamas under the fence to Bruno, who carefully changes into them, leaving his own clothes in a pile in the mud. The pajamas smell terrible. When Bruno shows Shmuel how he looks, Shmuel thinks to himself that if Bruno were a bit skinnier, it would have been difficult to tell them apart. Bruno tells Shmuel that dressing up in the pajamas reminds him of the plays he used to put on with his Grandmother and Gretel.

Shmuel tells Bruno that he has to remove his boots, too, or he will be recognized. His bare feet sink into the mud; at first this makes him uncomfortable, but then he begins to enjoy the feeling. Shmuel lifts the fence and Bruno shimmies underneath it, becoming quite muddy in the process. Each boy has the urge to hug the other, but neither does. They walk back to the populated part of the camp together and Bruno is surprised at how it looks. He had imagined happy families and children playing games together, shops, a town center, and people chatting.

But in contrast with what Bruno had envisioned, the people are just standing or sitting, "looking horribly sad" (207). They are all too skinny and have shaved heads, which Bruno takes to indicate that they have had lice here, too. Bruno notices that there are two groups of people: the soldiers, who seem to be having a happy time, and the people in the striped pajamas, who are cowering or crying. He tells Shmuel he doesn't like it there and wants to go home, but Shmuel reminds him that he promised he'd help look for his father. Bruno agrees and they spend an hour and a half searching for evidence. They don't find anything, which is what Shmuel had expected, and Bruno says again that he ought to go home.

Just then, the soldiers round up the people around Bruno and Shmuel. Shmuel reassures Bruno that "it happens sometimes... They make people go on marches" (210). Bruno is distressed because he doesn't have time to go on a march - he needs to be home for roast beef dinner. Shmuel tells him not to say anything because the soldiers will get angry, and Bruno obeys. He doesn't understand why all the other people marching with them look so frightened. Just as Bruno is beginning to lose patience and deciding that he really must go home because he is too cold, the group is marched into a warm, airtight room. Bruno apologizes to Shmuel that they weren't able to find his father, then tells him that when he comes to visit him in Berlin, they can spend time with all Bruno's old friends. He makes sure to tell Shmuel that he is his "best friend for life" (213). At that moment, the people in the room with them all gasp as the door is slammed shut and locked. The room becomes dark and chaotic, but Bruno and Shmuel continue to hold hands.

The soldiers search for Bruno for days his clothes and boots are discovered by the fence. Father goes to see them but cannot figure out what happened to his son. Mother and Gretel stay at Out-With for a few months waiting for news of Bruno. One day, Mother has the sudden notion that he might have returned to their home in Berlin, so she rushes back with Gretel but doesn't find Bruno there. Over the next year, Father becomes very disliked by all the soldiers at Out-With. Finally, he returns to the place where his son's clothes had been found and notices the opening in the fence. He realizes what must have happened, and a few months later he is discharged from his post at Out-With and taken away by soldiers.

Analysis

In Chapter Eighteen, the dramatic irony that has been at work throughout the story takes a tragic turn. The reader does not yet know what the terrible result of Bruno's last adventure will be, but the cliff hanger creates an ironic sense of doom: "[all] in all, it seemed like a very sensible plan and a good way to say goodbye" (199). The boys think this adventure will be their time to say goodbye to each other, when in reality they will be saying goodbye to the world. When the boys get rounded up and forced to march into the gas chamber with the group of Jews, Bruno is worried he won't be home in time for dinner and asks his friend if the marching usually goes on for long. Shmuel answers, "I never see the people after they've gone on a march. But I wouldn't imagine it does" (211). The reader knows that the reason he never sees the people is because they are being marched to their deaths in a gas chamber, but neither Shmuel nor Bruno understands this.

The details of the boys' deaths are omitted, which implies that they represent all the children who died during the Holocaust without completely understanding what was going on. The room they arrive in "felt completely airtight," something that is comforting to Bruno because he has been cold outdoors during the march (212). In fact, the room is airtight because it is a gas chamber. The reader has all doubt removed when the door to the chamber is slammed shut and the people in it gasp loudly. Bruno assumes "it had something to do with keeping the rain out and stopping people from catching colds" (213). When the boys die, they are holding hands, and Boyne doesn't specify whether they ever realize what is happening.

Bruno's limited perspective also comes into play in these last chapters, preventing him from understanding the fate he is about to experience in the gas chamber. As he is marched along with the other prisoners, "he [wants] to whisper to them that everything was all right, that Father was the Commandant, and if this was the kind of thing that he wanted the people to do then it must be all right" (210). Bruno is, of course, completely wrong: this *is* the sort of thing Father wants the Jews to do, but there is nothing "all right" about it. The very person in whom Bruno has faith is the one who is bringing about the deaths of so many, his own son included.

Shmuel's point of view is inserted into Chapter Eighteen deliberately, to further blur the distinction between the two boys. When Bruno asks him about whether he hates Bruno's Father in addition to all the other soldiers, Shmuel remains silent but thinks to himself about how "he had seen Bruno's father on any number of occasions and couldn't understand how such a man could have a son who was so friendly and kind" (196). The narrator remains in the third person, but reveals insight into Shmuel's thought process in a way which allows us the perspective of someone other than Bruno. When Bruno has put on the pajamas and turns around to show Shmuel what he looks like, "[it] was almost (Shmuel thought) as if they were all exactly the same really" (204). Boyne puts the indication of Shmuel's point of view in parentheses in order to imply that while the thought is Shmuel's, it is also a commentary on the situation generally. Once Bruno puts on the pajamas he looks no different from Shmuel; but really, the distinction made between the Jews and the Germans is arbitrary and erroneous, since they are all human beings.

In the last chapters, Boyne issues a veiled call to action to the reader, who might be living during a time of war or genocide. The most obvious instance is in the ironic tone on the final page of the story, when, after a devastated Father has been taken away from Out-With, the narrator says that "[of] course all this happened a long time ago and nothing like that could ever happen again. Not in this day and age" (216). Boyne means for the reader to consider just the opposite: there *are* genocides occurring in this day and age, all over the world, and the reader is likely employing various coping strategies to ignore or dismiss them. Bruno's annoyance at being forced to march with the group of Jews in the concentration camp is representative of the disconnect common to many witnesses of genocide. As Bruno is marched through the cold mud and rain, "he longed to be back in his house, watching all this from a distance and not wrapped up in the center of it" (211). This idea is a commentary on the perspective of those who allowed the Holocaust to occur while they remained removed from it, since it did not affect them personally. It applies to all witnesses to genocide in any time or place. The reader is meant to question how easy it is to watch from a distance, as long as one is not victimized.

The Boy in the Striped Pajamas The Boy in the Striped Pajamas: Film

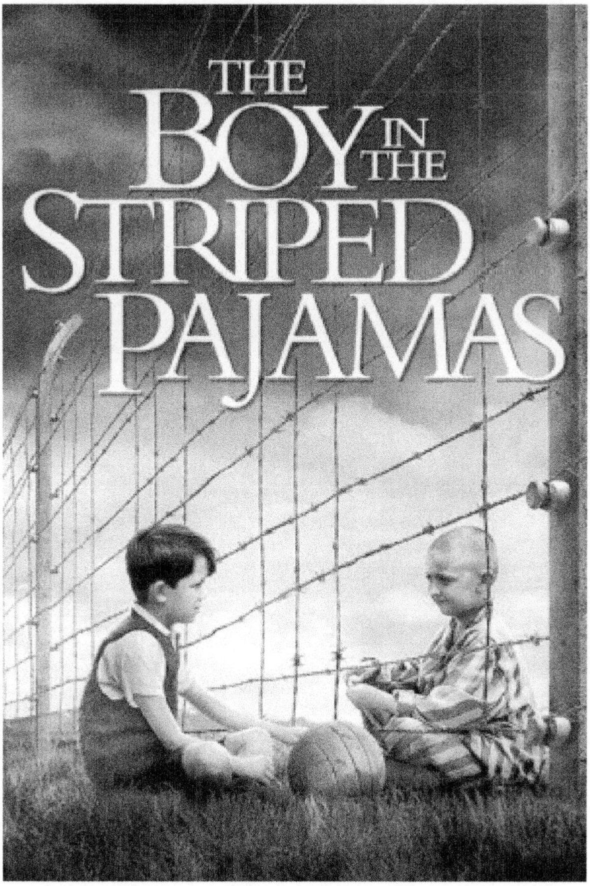

In 2008, Miramax Films released *The Boy in the Striped Pajamas*, directed by Mark Herman and starring Asa Butterfield as Bruno. Vera Farmiga was awarded the Best Actress British Independent Film Award for her portrayal of Bruno's mother, and Mark Heyman was nominated for Best Director. The film itself was nominated for a Premio Goya and an Irish Film and Television Award.

The film is quite loyal to Boyne's novel, with a few significant differences. The first is that Bruno is only eight years old in the film. The chapter in which The Fury comes to dinner with Eva at Bruno's family's house in Berlin is not represented in the film. Instead of this scene and other flashbacks that fill in information for the reader, the film begins with a large party scene at Bruno's family's home in Berlin.

The character of Mother is also different in the film: while in Boyne's novel, the extent to which she understand the atrocities of Auschwitz is unclear, in the film, she is completely unaware of the genocide. This makes her character more relatable to the viewer, since she is excused from the responsibility of participating in the Nazi movement.

The end of the film is also altered in order to heighten drama for the audience, as one might expect from any film adaptation. In Boyne's novel, the boys are gassed long before Bruno's clothes are found or the Commandant suspects that his son could become a victim of the Holocaust. In the film, shots of the boys being led to the gas chamber are interspersed with shots of Bruno's family searching for him, and when the gap in the fence is discovered, the audience is left with the impression that it is just barely too late to save Bruno's life.

The Boy in the Striped Pajamas Links

Films: John Boyne

http://www.johnboyne.com/films/

On his website, Boyne has compiled the trailers of all the films that have been made based on his novels and short stories.

The Boy in the Striped Pajamas Film Website

http://www.miramax.com/movie/the-boy-in-the-striped-pajamas/

This is the official site for the 2008 film adaptation of Boyne's novel.

The Boy in the Striped Pajamas Suggested Essays

1. **The experiences of women during wartimes have historically differed from those of men. How does Boyne use the character of Mother to explore this issue?**

   Father's literal silencing of Mother in most of their arguments and conversations is representative of the figurative silencing of women's voices in many times of war. At first, Mother reacts passive-aggressively, for example by referring to Father as "some people." She copes with the situation at Out-With by having an affair with Lieutenant Kotler. Father finds out and removes the young soldier, which sends Mother into a depression. She takes many afternoon naps, Bruno observes, and drinks what she calls "medicinal sherries." When Bruno overhears Mother confronting Father in Chapter Seventeen, she speaks up for herself and demands to leave Out-With. She tells Father, "This is your assignment, not ours. You stay if you want to" (187). At a time when gender roles determined that a wife obey her husband, this distinction between his responsibilities and her own is a bold statement.

2. **Boyne uses the tool of dramatic irony throughout the story. How does it manifest in the final chapters of the novel?**

   When the boys get rounded up and forced to march into the gas chamber with the group of Jews, Bruno is worried he won't be home in time for dinner and asks Shmuel if the marching usually goes on for long. Shmuel answers, "I never see the people after they've gone on a march. But I wouldn't imagine it does" (211). The reader knows that the reason he never sees the people is because they are being marched to their deaths in a gas chamber, but neither Shmuel nor Bruno is aware of this tragic information. As Bruno is marched along with the other prisoners, "he wanted to whisper to them that everything was all right, that Father was the Commandant, and if this was the kind of thing that he wanted the people to do then it must be all right" (210). Bruno is, of course, completely wrong: this is the sort of thing Father wants the Jews to do, but there is nothing "all right" about it. The very person in whom Bruno has faith is the one who is bringing about the deaths of so many, his own son included. The room they arrive in "felt completely airtight" (212), something that is comforting to Bruno because he has been feeling wet and cold outdoors during the march. In fact, the room is airtight because it is a gas chamber. The reader has all doubt removed when the door to the chamber is slammed shut and the people in it gasp loudly. Bruno assumes "it had something to do with keeping the rain out and stopping people from catching colds" (213). When the boys die, they are holding hands, and the narrator doesn't specify whether they ever realize what is happening.

3. **Why might Boyne have chosen to use a limited third-person narrator in the telling of this tragic story?**

   The limited narrator presents a childlike perception; Bruno thinks about things concretely and tries to make sense of rules and then apply them to all situations. For example, Bruno understands that Father's office is "Out Of Bounds At All Times And No Exceptions," a phrase that he has presumably memorized after hearing it many times from his parents. The reader is encouraged to take on this child-like point of view through the use of capitalization and the misnaming of specific people and places. Bruno refers to his father's boss as "the Fury"; the reader must extrapolate that this is actually "the Furor," or Adolf Hitler. Because of the limits of the narrator, the reader is able to approach the horrors of the Holocaust as if he or she has no prior knowledge - much like Bruno. The reader is required to put together details Bruno notices in order to make sense of the larger issues at play.

4. **How does Boyne bring the past into the present to create a sense of timelessness around the Holocaust?**

   The name "Out-With" is clearly a misunderstanding of the name "Auschwitz," but by refusing to name the concentration camp, Boyne avoids specificity to a certain extent. Bruno doesn't understand the derogatory term that Lieutenant Kotler calls Pavel and, later, Shmuel. By not specifically naming the word, Boyne suggests the universality of this interaction. Lieutenant Kotler could be any soldier during any war time, shouting a derogatory term to dehumanize a victim of any genocide. This provides the fable with a sense of timelessness, extending beyond the specific situation at Auschwitz. In the last chapters, Boyne issues a veiled call to action to the reader, who could be living during a time of war or genocide. The most obvious instance is in the ironic tone on the final page of the story, after a devastated Father has been taken away from Out-With: "Of course all this happened a long time ago and nothing like that could ever happen again. Not in this day and age" (216). Boyne means for the reader to consider just the opposite: there are genocides occurring in this day and age, all over the world, and the reader is likely employing various coping strategies to ignore or dismiss them.

5. **Discuss how the character of Gretel demonstrates the Nazi's indoctrination of children.**

   When Gretel is first introduced in Chapter Three, she is clearly a child, though a few years older than Bruno. She spends most of her time arranging her dolls and has brought the entire collection from Berlin with her. Significantly, she is the one who tells Bruno that the name of their new home is "Out-With." When Bruno points out how young she is in front of Lieutenant Kotler, she responds by snapping at him, "'I'll be thirteen in a couple of weeks' time. A teenager. Just like you'" (74). Her words to Lieutenant Kotler foreshadow her mental shift as she grows out of childhood. Eventually, Gretel replaces her collection of dolls with maps of Europe given to her by Father, which she updates using the newspapers each day as she reads about developments in the war. Her transition out of childhood naivete is represented clearly in her correction of Bruno's usage of "Out-With" in place of "Auschwitz." It was she who first told him the name of the place, but now she corrects him. Her understanding of the situation is still simplistic and lacks understanding: she has accepted what her Father and Herr Liszt have taught her without much critical thinking.

6. **One of the ways the Nazis defended their abhorrent actions against Jews was by arguing that the Aryan race was naturally "superior" to others. How does Boyne counter that claim?**

   Boyne introduces the theme of the natural world versus the unnaturalness of Auschwitz and the Holocaust in general. Instead of answering Bruno's question about whether she likes it at Out-With, Maria describes how much she loved the garden at the house in Berlin. Bruno takes this as an indirect answer to his question, since it is in such stark contrast to the atmosphere at Auschwitz. The theme of the Holocaust being unnatural arises again in Chapter Eleven, when Mother protests the move to Out-With by saying, "...as if it's the most natural thing in the world and it's not, it's just not..." (124). The Nazis used the argument that the Aryan race was "naturally" superior to all others, using the idea of natural dominance as justification in exterminating the Jewish population. But Boyne turns this assumption on its head, pointing out throughout the story just how unnatural the atmosphere and situation at Out-With really is.

7. **What purpose does Father's transformation at the end of the story serve?**

   In the final pages of the story, Father realizes that Bruno has gone to the other side of the fence and must have been killed in a gas chamber. When the atrocities that he has been routinely committing against other people's children happen to his own child, he has a different perspective on the situation. Until that point, he has been convincing himself that the Jews are not real people. He assures Bruno that the Jews on the other side of the fence are "not people at all" - this is how he justifies to himself the systematic killing of them at Auschwitz (53). Maria's description of how kind Father has been to her serves as a commentary on the mental and emotional justification for Nazi soldiers generally, who might do kind deeds and appear to be wonderful people in other parts of their lives, yet also are responsible for the extermination of Jews.

8. **How does Boyne use specific actions to represent the larger idea of complacency with regard to the Holocaust?**

Bruno's betrayal of Shmuel in front of Lieutenant Kotler is representative of the many people who betrayed their Jewish neighbors and friends during the Holocaust in similar ways, simply by being complacent. By distancing himself from Shmuel because he is afraid of the consequences of associating with the boy, Bruno contributes to Shmuel's punishment for a crime he did not commit: stealing food. The way Bruno relates to his actions immediately following the event reflects a personal disconnect: "[he] wondered how a boy who thought he was a good person really could act in such a cowardly way toward a friend" (174). He feels ashamed of himself, but does not take action to right the wrong. When Shmuel finally returns to meet him at the fence, his face covered in bruises, Bruno apologizes. His words could have easily come from any of the Germans who fell in line with the Nazis and didn't speak up for the Jews during the Holocaust. Likewise, when Lieutenant Kotler attacks Pavel for accidentally spilling the wine, the narrator only states that "[what] happened then was both unexpected and extremely unpleasant. Lieutenant Kotler grew very angry with Pavel and no one - not Bruno, not Gretel, not Mother and not even Father - stepped in to stop him doing what he did next, even though none of them could watch" (148-49). This omission of detail makes the interaction representative of all acts of violence against Jews at the hands of Nazis; it also can be universalized to the oppressed group in any genocide throughout history. Bruno and his family represent the bystanders who were repulsed by did not act to stop the violence.

9. **The fence between Bruno and Shmuel is a literal boundary, but it serves a figurative purpose as well. Discuss how the fence functions as a symbol of arbitrary boundaries between people.**

The most obvious boundary in the story is the fence separating Bruno's side of Out-With from Shmuel's side; but Boyne calls into question the arbitrary boundaries that got each boy to his side of the fence: most importantly, that between Jews and "Opposites." The symbols of the Star of David and the Nazi Swastika, which are never named, come to represent the arbitrary boundary that allowed the Nazis to exterminate other human beings when the boys draw them in the dirt on either side of the fence. In Chapter Twelve, Shmuel describes how he came to have to wear his Star of David armband and draws the symbol in the dirt. Bruno points out that his Father wears one, too, and draws the Nazi symbol in the dirt on his side of the fence. The key difference between them is that Shmuel is Jewish and thus a member of the oppressed group in this genocide, while Bruno happens to be German and thus a member of the oppressive group. When Bruno tells Shmuel that Father also wears an armband, Shmuel observes, "[yes], but they're different, aren't they?" (127).

10. **Boyne uses a third-person narrator to tell the story mostly from Bruno's perspective. At times, the perspective shifts to represent Shmuel's point of view. What is the purpose of this tactic?**

Shmuel serves as a mirror character for Bruno; they were born on the same day, and Bruno declares, "[we're] like twins" (110). The use of Shmuel's point of view functions as a way to blur the boundary between the two boys. When Bruno has put on the pajamas and turns around to show Shmuel what he looks like, "[it] was almost (Shmuel thought) as if they were all exactly the same really" (204). Boyne puts the indication of Shmuel's point of view in parentheses in order to imply that while the thought is Shmuel's, it is also a commentary on the situation generally. Once Bruno puts on the pajamas he looks no different from Shmuel, but really, the distinction made between the Jews and the Germans is arbitrary and erroneous, since they are all human beings.

The Boy in the Striped Pajamas Quizzes

1. **Who does Bruno find packing his things at his home in Berlin?**
   A. Maria
   B. Pavel
   C. Gretel
   D. Mother

2. **What is the passive aggressive term Mother uses to refer to Father?**
   A. "some people"
   B. "my dear husband"
   C. "that man"
   D. "he who must be obeyed"

3. **Which is not the name of one of Bruno's friends in Berlin?**
   A. Shmuel
   B. Daniel
   C. Karl
   D. Martin

4. **According to Bruno, what is the best thing about the house in Berlin?**
   A. His bedroom
   B. The attic
   C. The bannister
   D. The backyard garden

5. **Which room is Out of Bounds At All Times And No Exceptions?**
   A. Gretel's room
   B. The balcony
   C. Mother's bathroom
   D. Father's office

6. **What is not true about the new house?**
   A. It is very close to the houses on either side of it.
   B. It has three floors.
   C. It has no neighboring houses.
   D. It gives Bruno a sad feeling.

7. **How long does Gretel tell Bruno she thinks they will have to stay at the new house?**
   A. For years
   B. Just for that night
   C. For the afternoon
   D. For "the foreseeable future"

8. **Who helps Bruno unpack his belongings in the new home?**
   A. Lieutenant Kotler
   B. Maria
   C. Mother
   D. Pavel

9. **Who walks by Bruno's bedroom door on the first day they arrive at their new house?**
   A. Shmuel
   B. Pavel
   C. Father
   D. Lieutenant Kotler

10. **What does Bruno call Gretel?**
   A. The Horrible Girl
   B. Meanie
   C. The Hopeless Case
   D. Sister Dearest

11. **What collection has Gretel brought with her from Berlin?**
   A. maps
   B. bottle caps
   C. stamps
   D. dolls

12. **Why did Gretel's friends in Berlin make fun of Bruno?**
   A. Because he is small for his age.
   B. Because he is not as smart as the other children.
   C. Because he can't run quickly.
   D. Because he is fat.

13. **Who tells Bruno that their new home is called Out-With?**
   A. Shmuel
   B. Gretel
   C. Father
   D. Maria

14. **What is not one of the names of Gretel's friends in Berlin?**
   A. Maria
   B. Hilda
   C. Louise
   D. Isobel

15. **What does Bruno tell Gretel about the other children at Out-With?**
   A. They look too skinny.
   B. They live in the basement.
   C. There are none.
   D. They don't look at all friendly.

16. **What can be seen out of the window in Gretel's room?**
   A. A high wall.
   B. The concentration camp.
   C. The driveway and a forest beyond it.
   D. The ocean.

17. **What can be seen out of the window in Bruno's room?**
   A. The car.
   B. Lieutenant Kotler's house.
   C. A garden and beyond it, the concentration camp.
   D. The city of Cracow.

18. **What is Gretel's first explanation for the view from Bruno's room?**
   A. It is a concentration camp.
   B. It is the countryside.
   C. It is a war.
   D. It is a summer camp.

19. **Who arrived at Out-With first?**
   A. Bruno
   B. Father
   C. Mother
   D. Maria

20. **What event does Mother blame for their move to Out-With?**
   A. Father's affair with another woman.
   B. The fight with Grandmother.
   C. The Fury coming to dinner.
   D. The beginning of the war.

21. **Who overhears Mother complaining as they leave the house in Berlin?**
   A. Cook
   B. Father
   C. Maria
   D. Grandmother

22. **What does Bruno see at the train station?**
   A. An execution.
   B. Another, much more crowded train headed the same direction.
   C. Soldiers having a fight.
   D. A horse and carriage.

23. **Where does Bruno have his first conversation with Father at Out-With?**
   A. In Father's office.
   B. In his own bedroom.
   C. In the garden.
   D. On the other side of the fence.

24. **What does Bruno ask Father when they first arrive at Out-With?**

A. If and when they can move back to Berlin.

B. What time dinner will be served.

C. Why Lieutenant Kotler is in their home so much.

D. If he can build a tire swing.

25. **What does Father do while Bruno talks to him in the office?**

A. Sings a song Grandmother used to perform.

B. Starts a fight with mother.

C. Smokes a cigarette.

D. Drinks a medicinal sherry.

Quiz 1 Answer Key

1. **(A)** Maria
2. **(A)** "some people"
3. **(A)** Shmuel
4. **(C)** The bannister
5. **(D)** Father's office
6. **(A)** It is very close to the houses on either side of it.
7. **(D)** For "the foreseeable future"
8. **(B)** Maria
9. **(D)** Lieutenant Kotler
10. **(C)** The Hopeless Case
11. **(D)** dolls
12. **(A)** Because he is small for his age.
13. **(B)** Gretel
14. **(A)** Maria
15. **(D)** They don't look at all friendly.
16. **(C)** The driveway and a forest beyond it.
17. **(C)** A garden and beyond it, the concentration camp.
18. **(B)** It is the countryside.
19. **(B)** Father
20. **(C)** The Fury coming to dinner.
21. **(C)** Maria
22. **(B)** Another, much more crowded train headed the same direction.
23. **(A)** In Father's office.
24. **(A)** If and when they can move back to Berlin.
25. **(C)** Smokes a cigarette.

The Boy in the Striped Pajamas Quizzes

1. **What does Father tell Bruno about the people on the other side of the fence?**
   A. "They all have done something horrible."
   B. "We must kill them immediately."
   C. "They don't exist."
   D. "They're not people at all."

2. **What does Father remind Bruno to do before he leaves the office?**
   A. Bow.
   B. Salute.
   C. Thank his mother.
   D. Tie his shoes.

3. **What phrase does Bruno assume means, "Well, goodbye for now, have a pleasant afternoon"?**
   A. "Jew"
   B. "Some people."
   C. "Heil Hilter."
   D. "Out-With."

4. **What was Maria's favorite part of the house in Berlin?**
   A. The garden
   B. Her bedroom
   C. The neighborhood
   D. The piano

5. **What was Maria's mother's job?**
   A. A waitress
   B. A prostitute
   C. A dressmaker for Grandmother
   D. A doctor

6. **Who paid for Maria's mother's hospital care and funeral?**
   A. Lieutenant Kotler
   B. Mother
   C. Father
   D. Maria

7. **What does Gretel demand of Maria?**
    A. To run her a bath.
    B. To build her a tire swing.
    C. To leave her alone with Lieutenant Kotler.
    D. To organize her dolls for her.

8. **What does Maria advise Bruno to do about his dissatisfaction at Out-With?**
    A. Stay in his room and cry.
    B. Stay quiet about it.
    C. Speak up about his specific problems.
    D. Go exploring and have fun.

9. **What happened to make Herr Roller go mad?**
    A. He fell off a cliff.
    B. He lost his wife.
    C. He had syphilis.
    D. He suffered from a head injury during the Great War.

10. **Who scolds Bruno for laughing at Herr Roller?**
    A. Mother
    B. Gretel
    C. Isobel
    D. Father

11. **With whom is Gretel flirting on the day Bruno builds a tire swing?**
    A. Pavel
    B. Lieutenant Kotler
    C. Shmuel
    D. Martin

12. **Who accompanies Bruno to the storage shed to find a tire for his swing?**
    A. Pavel
    B. Father
    C. Lieutenant Kotler
    D. Maria

13. **How does Bruno injure himself?**
    A. Lieutenant Kotler punches him.
    B. He falls off the tire swing.
    C. He falls out the window.
    D. He cuts himself on the fence.

14. **What does Pavel do in Bruno's family's house?**
    A. Washes and folds the laundry.
    B. Sweeps the floors.
    C. Keeps guard.
    D. Peels vegetables and serves dinner.

15. **Who cleans Bruno's knee?**
    A. Father
    B. Maria
    C. Mother
    D. Pavel

16. **What does Mother tell Pavel she is going to take credit for?**
    A. Fixing the tire swing.
    B. Making dinner.
    C. Cleaning Bruno's knee.
    D. Spilling the wine.

17. **What was Pavel's profession before coming to Out-With?**
    A. Waiter
    B. Doctor
    C. Grocer
    D. Mechanic

18. **What does Bruno tell Pavel he wants to be when he grows up?**
    A. A soldier
    B. An explorer
    C. A doctor
    D. A waiter

19. **What was Grandmother's profession?**
    A. A soldier
    B. A nurse
    C. A singer
    D. A teacher

20. **What activity does Grandmother often do with Bruno and Gretel?**
    A. Put on dramatic productions
    B. Learn languages
    C. Go shopping
    D. Go fishing

21. **When was the last time Bruno saw his Grandmother?**
    A. On her visit to Out-With
    B. At his school graduation
    C. At their summer home
    D. On Christmas Day

22. **Who is outspoken about their disapproval of Father's job?**

A. Grandmother
B. Bruno
C. Maria
D. Grandfather

23. **To whom does Bruno write a letter from Out-With?**

A. Grandmother
B. Daniel
C. Martin
D. Grandfather

24. **Who is Herr Liszt?**

A. The tutor Father hires to teach Gretel and Bruno.
B. A soldier.
C. The man with whom Mother has an affair.
D. The Commandant who replaces Father.

25. **What subjects does Herr Liszt teach most?**

A. Math and science
B. History and geography
C. Languages
D. Art and music

Quiz 2 Answer Key

1. **(D)** "They're not people at all."
2. **(B)** Salute.
3. **(C)** "Heil Hilter."
4. **(A)** The garden
5. **(C)** A dressmaker for Grandmother
6. **(C)** Father
7. **(A)** To run her a bath.
8. **(B)** Stay quiet about it.
9. **(D)** He suffered from a head injury during the Great War.
10. **(A)** Mother
11. **(B)** Lieutenant Kotler
12. **(A)** Pavel
13. **(B)** He falls off the tire swing.
14. **(D)** Peels vegetables and serves dinner.
15. **(D)** Pavel
16. **(C)** Cleaning Bruno's knee.
17. **(B)** Doctor
18. **(B)** An explorer
19. **(C)** A singer
20. **(A)** Put on dramatic productions
21. **(D)** On Christmas Day
22. **(A)** Grandmother
23. **(A)** Grandmother
24. **(A)** The tutor Father hires to teach Gretel and Bruno.
25. **(B)** History and geography

The Boy in the Striped Pajamas Quizzes

1. **What is on the bench outside Bruno's house in Out-With?**
   A. A plaque
   B. A statue
   C. A group of birds
   D. A homeless person

2. **Where does Bruno first meet Shmuel?**
   A. In Berlin.
   B. Outside, through the fence.
   C. In Father's office.
   D. In his kitchen.

3. **What do Shmuel and Bruno have in common?**
   A. They share a birthday.
   B. They're both Jewish.
   C. They both speak Polish.
   D. They're both from Berlin.

4. **What does Bruno tell Shmuel about Germans?**
   A. "We are very similar to the Jews."
   B. "We are the master race."
   C. "There are too many of us."
   D. "We're superior."

5. **Who accompanies the Fury to dinner at Bruno's home in Berlin?**
   A. Eva
   B. Herr Roller
   C. Grandmother
   D. Lieutenant Kotler

6. **What does Father tell Bruno and Gretel to do during the Fury's visit?**
   A. Only speak when spoken to.
   B. Serve dinner to the adults.
   C. Only speak in French.
   D. Tell as many stories as they like.

7. **What stands out to Bruno about the Fury?**
   A. His tiny moustache
   B. His kind demeanor
   C. His large stature
   D. His small hands

8. **What is Bruno's impression of the Fury?**
    A. He never meets the Fury.
    B. That he is humble and kind.
    C. That he is terrifying and awe-inspiring.
    D. That he is a rude, horrible man.

9. **Who is the Fury?**
    A. Gretel
    B. Grandmother
    C. Father
    D. Adolf Hitler

10. **What does Shmuel tell Bruno the soldiers took from him?**
    A. His favorite shoes
    B. His doll
    C. All his books
    D. The watch his father made for him

11. **What does Bruno draw in the dirt on his side of the fence?**
    A. A swastika
    B. A cross
    C. His name
    D. A Star of David

12. **What did Shmuel's mother make for him and his family to wear?**
    A. Pajamas
    B. Armbands
    C. Jackets
    D. Hats

13. **What city did Shmuel live in before coming to Out-With?**
    A. New York
    B. Cracow
    C. Berlin
    D. Paris

14. **What does Shmuel ask Bruno for at their first meeting?**
    A. A book
    B. Clothes
    C. A watch
    D. Food

15. **Who tells Bruno about Pavel's history?**
    A. Maria
    B. Shmuel
    C. Mother
    D. Father

16. **What does Shmuel tell Bruno he wants to do when he grows up?**
    A. Fight in wars.
    B. Work in a zoo.
    C. Be a doctor.
    D. Explore.

17. **Who does Shmuel tell Bruno he doesn't like to talk about?**
    A. His own father
    B. Lieutenant Kotler
    C. Himself
    D. His mother

18. **What was Lieutenant Kotler's father's profession?**
    A. University professor
    B. Doctor
    C. Soldier
    D. Waiter

19. **What upsets Father at dinner with Lieutenant Kotler?**
    A. Gretel's flirting with Lieutenant Kotler.
    B. The weather.
    C. The fact that Lieutenant Kotler's father left Germany in 1938.
    D. Pavel's spilling of the wine.

20. **How old is Lieutenant Kotler?**
    A. Nineteen
    B. Fifteen
    C. Forty
    D. Twenty-eight

21. **What happens that prompts Lieutenant Kotler to attack Pavel?**
    A. Nothing
    B. Pavel spills wine on him
    C. Pavel slips and falls
    D. Pavel breaks the tire swing

22. **Who stands up for Pavel when Lieutenant Kotler attacks him?**
    A. Father
    B. Bruno
    C. Mother
    D. No one

23. **How does Bruno cover his mistake in telling Gretel about Shmuel?**
    A. He says Shmuel is a dog.
    B. He says Shmuel died.
    C. He says she misheard him and he didn't mention anything.
    D. He says Shmuel is his imaginary friend.

24. **For whom does Mother plan a birthday party?**
    A. Gretel
    B. Bruno
    C. Father
    D. Lieutenant Kotler

25. **With whom does Mother have an affair?**
    A. Lars
    B. Lieutenant Kotler
    C. Herr Roller
    D. Pavel

Quiz 3 Answer Key

1. **(A)** A plaque
2. **(B)** Outside, through the fence.
3. **(A)** They share a birthday.
4. **(D)** "We're superior."
5. **(A)** Eva
6. **(A)** Only speak when spoken to.
7. **(A)** His tiny moustache
8. **(D)** That he is a rude, horrible man.
9. **(D)** Adolf Hitler
10. **(D)** The watch his father made for him
11. **(A)** A swastika
12. **(B)** Armbands
13. **(B)** Cracow
14. **(D)** Food
15. **(A)** Maria
16. **(B)** Work in a zoo.
17. **(B)** Lieutenant Kotler
18. **(A)** University professor
19. **(C)** The fact that Lieutenant Kotler's father left Germany in 1938.
20. **(A)** Nineteen
21. **(B)** Pavel spills wine on him
22. **(D)** No one
23. **(D)** He says Shmuel is his imaginary friend.
24. **(C)** Father
25. **(B)** Lieutenant Kotler

The Boy in the Striped Pajamas Quizzes

1. **What book does Lieutenant Kotler snatch out of Bruno's hands?**
   A. The Bible
   B. A Tale of Two Cities
   C. Alice in Wonderland
   D. Treasure Island

2. **What is Shmuel supposed to be doing in the kitchen?**
   A. Cooking
   B. Helping Pavel peel the vegetables
   C. Polishing the glasses for the party
   D. Sleeping

3. **What does Mother drink?**
   A. Water
   B. Medicinal sherries
   C. Wine
   D. Whiskey

4. **What does Bruno feed Shmuel in the kitchen?**
   A. Cold chicken
   B. Nothing
   C. Bread and cheese
   D. Cake

5. **What does Bruno say when Lieutenant Kotler asks him if Shmuel is his friend?**
   A. "I would never be friends with a Jew."
   B. "Yes, we're friends."
   C. "I've never seen him before in my life. I don't know him."
   D. "No, I hate him!"

6. **When do the boys first touch each other?**
   A. In Father's office.
   B. When Bruno comes over to Shmuel's side of the fence.
   C. In the kitchen of Bruno's house.
   D. When they shake hands under the fence after Bruno apologizes to Shmuel.

7. **For what occasion does Bruno's family briefly return to Berlin?**
   A. Mother's birthday
   B. Father's book release
   C. Grandmother's funeral
   D. To sell the house

8. **Who leaves Out-With suddenly after a fight between Father and Mother?**
   A. Grandfather
   B. Lieutenant Kotler
   C. Gretel
   D. Shmuel

9. **What does Gretel do with her dolls eventually?**
   A. Burns them.
   B. Gives them to the children on the other side of the fence.
   C. Sends them back to Berlin.
   D. Throws them all away.

10. **What does Gretel find in her hair?**
    A. A spider
    B. A bow
    C. A tiny egg
    D. A patch of grey hairs

11. **Who shaves Bruno's head?**
    A. Pavel
    B. Shmuel
    C. Father
    D. Bruno

12. **What explanation does Bruno have for Shmuel's father's disappearance?**
    A. That he escaped.
    B. That he was taken to another town to work for a few days.
    C. That he has been killed.
    D. That he left to return to Cracow.

13. **What does Shmuel ask Bruno to do with him on the other side of the fence?**
    A. Have a footrace.
    B. Help him look for his father.
    C. Play hopscotch.
    D. Dig a tunnel.

14. **What is the weather like on the Friday Bruno sneaks under the fence?**
    A. It is rainy and muddy.
    B. It is snowing.
    C. It is a beautiful, sunny day.
    D. It is overcast but very warm.

15. **Where does Bruno leave his clothes when he sneaks under the fence?**
    A. He buries them under a tree.
    B. In a plastic bag he's brought from home.
    C. He hangs them on the fence.
    D. In a pile in the mud.

16. **What does dressing up in the striped pajamas remind Bruno of?**
    A. Playing dress-up with his friends from school.
    B. Going to bed.
    C. Putting on plays with Grandmother.
    D. Halloween.

17. **What evidence do Bruno and Shmuel find in relation to Shmuel's father's disappearance?**
    A. A watch.
    B. None.
    C. A letter.
    D. A pile of abandoned clothes.

18. **What do the soldiers make Bruno and Shmuel do?**
    A. Go on a march.
    B. Hide.
    C. Dig a hole.
    D. Stand in a straight line.

19. **What happens to Bruno and Shmuel at the end of the story?**
    A. They say goodbye and see each other years later in Berlin.
    B. They escape from Out-With.
    C. They die in a gas chamber.
    D. They grow up to become explorers.

20. **Who finds Bruno's abandoned clothes and boots?**
    A. Mother
    B. A soldier
    C. Father
    D. Gretel

21. **How long does Father stay at Out-With after Bruno's disappearance?**
    A. A year
    B. One day
    C. Many years
    D. A few weeks

22. **Why does Father collapse at the side of the fence?**

A. He has broken his legs.
B. He is out of breath from running.
C. He has a heart attack.
D. He realizes what has happened to Bruno.

23. **How does Gretel react to Bruno's disappearance?**

A. She won't speak for weeks.
B. She cries in her room alone.
C. She becomes obsessed with her dolls.
D. She runs away from home.

24. **How does Father react when he is removed from his post at Out-With?**

A. He is furious.
B. He appeals to the Fury for a new appointment.
C. He is relieved because he has been wanting to return to Berlin.
D. He doesn't care because he doesn't care what happens to him anymore.

25. **Why does Mother suddenly return to Berlin?**

A. She is violently ill and needs to rest in a comfortable place.
B. She has the idea that Bruno might have returned to their home there.
C. She thinks Lieutenant Kotler might be there.
D. She wants to sell the house.

Quiz 4 Answer Key

1. **(D)** Treasure Island
2. **(C)** Polishing the glasses for the party
3. **(B)** Medicinal sherries
4. **(A)** Cold chicken
5. **(C)** "I've never seen him before in my life. I don't know him."
6. **(D)** When they shake hands under the fence after Bruno apologizes to Shmuel.
7. **(C)** Grandmother's funeral
8. **(B)** Lieutenant Kotler
9. **(D)** Throws them all away.
10. **(C)** A tiny egg
11. **(C)** Father
12. **(B)** That he was taken to another town to work for a few days.
13. **(B)** Help him look for his father.
14. **(A)** It is rainy and muddy.
15. **(D)** In a pile in the mud.
16. **(C)** Putting on plays with Grandmother.
17. **(B)** None.
18. **(A)** Go on a march.
19. **(C)** They die in a gas chamber.
20. **(B)** A soldier
21. **(A)** A year
22. **(D)** He realizes what has happened to Bruno.
23. **(B)** She cries in her room alone.
24. **(D)** He doesn't care because he doesn't care what happens to him anymore.
25. **(B)** She has the idea that Bruno might have returned to their home there.

The Boy in the Striped Pajamas Bibliography

Meghan Joyce Tozer, author of ClassicNote. Completed on May 11, 2014, copyright held by GradeSaver.

Updated and revised by Aaron Suduiko October 26, 2014. Copyright held by GradeSaver.

Reynolds, Kimberly. Children's Literature: A Very Short Introduction. Oxford, New York: Oxford University Press, 2011.

Bayer, Gerd. "World War II Fiction and the Ethics of Trauma" in "Ethics and Trauma in Contemporary British Fiction," eds. Susana Onega and Jean-Michel Ganteau. Amsterdam, New York: Rodopi, 2011.

"Irish Writers Online." 2014-04-28. <http://www.irishwriters-online.com/boyne-john/>.

"John Boyne." 2014-04-28. <http://www.johnboyne.com>.

Roy, Karen. "John Boyne Interview." The View From Here Magazine. 2014-04-28. <http://www.viewfromheremagazine.com/2012/01/john-boyne-interview.html>.

Burling, Alexis. "Author Interview: John Boyne." TeenReads.com. 2014-04-28. <http://www.teenreads.com/authors/john-boyne/news/interview-090906>.

John Boyne. "John Boyne Writer." 2014-04-28. <http://johnboynewriter.wordpress.com/>.

Essay Trying Themes of 'The Boy in the Striped Pajamas'

by Anonymous

John Boyne's most famous novel, The Boy in the Striped Pajamas, is an intricate story about two boys that meet at a concentration camp during the Second World War. In this novel, several themes are made evident, such as the innocence of childhood, prejudices, fear, regret, and boundaries. However, perhaps the most interesting, yet subtle, theme is that of silence.

Silence, stillness, and secrets are all interconnected throughout this literary work. As the protagonist's father is the "Commandment" of the German army, the majority of his duties are hidden from his family. This is taken to such extremes that the family moves to Poland, without telling the children where they are moving to or the reason behind it. There is an overall silence throughout the family, particularly when it comes to the work of the father. The children are taught at an early age to simply respect his duties and to not question his decisions.

As the story continues, Bruno develops a close friendship with a refugee named Shmuel. Shmuel is the Hebrew equivalent of the name Samuel, meaning strong. This fact is quite interesting in relation to Shmuel's role in the story, particularly in his role in the friendship between the two boys. Due to the differences between the two, Bruno is required to not mention his new friendship to anyone. After he makes a Freudian slip in a conversation with his sister, Bruno is forced to cover his tracks: "' I have a new friend,' he began. 'A new friend that I go to see every day. And he'll be waiting for me now. But you can't tell anyone.' 'Why not?' 'Because he's an imaginary friend,' said Bruno, trying his best to look embarrassed…" (155). unfortunately, this is not the only time that Bruno lies about his relationship with Shmuel. While the two are talking when Shmuel comes to clean out the glasses in Bruno's kitchen, they are caught by Lieutenant Kotler. Shmuel easily admits that the two are friends, while Bruno claims to have never spoken with or seen Shmuel in his life. However, his decision to cover up their friendship does not sit well with him: "[Bruno's] stomach churned inside him and he thought for a moment that he was going to be sick. He had never felt so ashamed in his life; he had never imagined that he could behave so cruelly. He wondered how a boy who thought he was a good person really could act in such a cowardly way towards a friend" (173–174). While the two young boys do not have a thorough understanding of their situations, they are intelligent enough to know that there is something more powerful than a fence that is keeping them apart. Hyde made an interesting point regarding this scene: "This incident suggests how silence imposed from the outside – by Lieutenant Kotler's intimidating and threatening presence – could act so as to stifle Bruno's sense of agency and his spirituality, thereby leading to a sense of disconnectedness with his friend Shmuel" (98).

By contrast, silence and stillness are not always portrayed as negative things in this novel. Near the end of the book, Bruno disguises himself in the "striped pyjamas" and attempts to assist Shmuel in finding his father. When the soldiers gathered up the Jews for their march, Bruno took a great step of boldness in regards to their friendship: "He looked down and did something quite out of character for him: he took hold of Shmuel's tiny hand in his and squeezed it tightly. 'You're my best friend, Shmuel,' he said. 'My best friend for life'" (212-213). While the boys remained in the gas chamber, not knowing what to expect, they still clung to each other: "…the room went very dark and somehow, despite the chaos that followed, Bruno found that he was still holding Shmuel's hand in his own and nothing in the world would have persuaded him to let it go" (213). Hyde's statement on this scene was quite intriguing:" Of all the ways in which they could have reacted in the midst of the chaos and the horror that was about to take place, Bruno and Shmuel chose silence. They stood holding hands, affirming their connectedness (irrespective of their very different racial backgrounds)…" (98). This scene represents the fact that silence has a strange power over words and that it is not always necessarily to speak in order to communicate.

The innocence of a child and the power of silence in both positive and negative aspects are recurrent themes throughout John Boyne's The Boy in the Striped Pajamas. Boyne does an excellent job describing the relationships that Bruno has with his family and with his new friend Shmuel. The two boys are wise for their ages, as they have the power to look beyond the things that separate them and to form a bond that words cannot break. These two young boys are a great example of true friendship and overcoming obstacles.

Hyde, Brendan, Karen-Marie Yust, and Cathy Ota. "Silence, Agency And Spiritual

Development." International Journal Of Children's Spirituality 15.2 (2010): 97-99. Academic Search Premier. Web. 8 Feb. 2013.

ClassicNotes

GradeSaver™

Getting you the grade since 1999™

Other ClassicNotes from GradeSaver™

Emily Dickinson's Collected Poems
Emma
Ender's Game
Endgame
Enduring Love
Enrique's Journey
Esperanza Rising
Eternal Sunshine of the Spotless Mind
Ethan Frome
Evelina
Everyday Use
Everyman: Morality Play
Everything is Illuminated
Exeter Book
Extremely Loud and Incredibly Close
Ezra Pound: Poems
Fahrenheit 451
Fallen Angels
Fear and Loathing in Las Vegas
Fences
Fifth Business
Fight Club
Fight Club (Film)
Flags of Our Fathers
Flannery O'Connor's Stories
Flight
For Colored Girls Who Have Considered Suicide When the Rainbow Is Enuf
For Whom the Bell Tolls
Founding Brothers
Frankenstein
Franny and Zooey
Friday Night Lights
Fun Home
Goethe's Faust
Gorilla, My Love
Great Expectations
Grendel
Gulliver's Travels
Hamlet
Hard Times
Haroun and the Sea of Stories
Harry Potter and the Philosopher's Stone
Heart of Darkness
Hedda Gabler
Henry IV Part 1
Henry IV Part 2
Henry IV (Pirandello)
Henry V
Herzog
Hippolytus
Homo Faber
House of Mirth

For our full list of over 250 Study Guides, Quizzes,
Sample College Application Essays, Literature Essays and E-texts, visit:

www.gradesaver.com

ClassicNotes

GradeSaver™

Getting you the grade since 1999™

Other ClassicNotes from GradeSaver™

The House of Bernarda Alba
The House of the Seven Gables
The House of the Spirits
The Hunger Games
The Importance of Being Earnest
Their Eyes Were Watching God
The Island of Dr. Moreau
The Jew of Malta
The Joy Luck Club
The Jungle
The Kite Runner
The Lais of Marie de France
The Legend of Sleepy Hollow
The Life of Olaudah Equiano
The Lion, the Witch and the Wardrobe
The Lone Ranger and Tonto Fistfight in Heaven
The Lord of the Rings: The Fellowship of the Ring
The Lord of the Rings: The Return of the King
The Lord of the Rings: The Two Towers
The Lottery and Other Stories
The Lovely Bones
The Love Song of J. Alfred Prufrock
The Marrow of Tradition
The Master and Margarita
The Mayor of Casterbridge
The Maze Runner
The Metamorphosis
The Mill on the Floss
The Most Dangerous Game
The Namesake
The Narrative of Arthur Gordon Pym of Nantucket
The Odyssey
The Old Man and the Sea
The Origin of Species
The Outsiders
The Pearl
The Perks of Being a Wallflower

For our full list of over 250 Study Guides, Quizzes, Sample College Application Essays, Literature Essays and E-texts, visit:

www.gradesaver.com

Printed in Great Britain
by Amazon

35992732R00061